For information on how you can have *Better Homes & Gardens* magazine delivered to your door, write to:
Robert Austin, P.O. Box 4536, Des Moines, IA 50336.

Editor: Diana Deakin
Design and Production: Judy Clark
Illustrations: Constance Daly
Photography: Evan Bracken for Cuddly Bear, Sweetheart Bear, Treasure Bear, Backpack, and all how-to photos.
All other photos: © Ariadne/Eska Tijdschriften B.V., Utrecht, Holland.
Technical Assistance: Elaine McPherson and her entire staff at A Stitch 'n Time

Special thanks to Kate Mathews for her professional advice and Elaine McPherson for her many hours of technical assistance.

Cuddly Bear, Treasure Bear, and Sweetheart Bear were designed, made, written, and provided by Elaine McPherson.

Library of Congress Cataloging-in-Publication Data
The Bear Book: Teddy bears and a few close friends
Edited by Diana Deakin.
        p.   cm.
    ISBN 8-8069-5820-0
    1. Soft toy making.   2. Teddy bears   I. Deakin, Diana.
    TT174.3.B43   1990
    745.592'4--dc20
                                                89-21899
10 9 8 7 6 5 4 3 2 1   CIP

A Sterling/Lark Book

Produced by Altamont Press, Inc.
50 College Street, Asheville, NC 28801, USA

Published in 1990 by Sterling Publishing Co., Inc.
387 Park Avenue South, New York, NY 10016

Distributed in Canada by Sterling Publishing
c/o Canadian Manda Group, P.O. Box 920, Station U
Toronto, Ontario, Canada M8Z 5P9
Distributed in the United Kingdom by Cassell PLC
Villiers House, 41/47 Strand, London WC2N 5JE, England
Distributed in Australia by Capricorn, Ltd.,
P.O. Box 665, Lane Cove, NSW 2066

Printed in Hong Kong

The Bear Book

Edited by Diana Deakin

A Sterling/ **Lark** book
Sterling Publishing Co., Inc., New York

Contents

Teddy Bears—Their Place in History 6

Bear Necessities 9

Cuddly Bear 29

Olaf and Ollie 30

Sweetheart Bear 32

Panda Bear 33

Brown Bear 34

Petie Polar Bear 35

Max 36

Corduroy Bear 53

Treasure Bear 54

Best Friend Bear 56

Bear Scarf and Mittens 89

Bear Purse 90

Bear Cushion 91

Bear Hanger 92

Cross-Stitched Hat Rack 93

Scarf and Muffler Set 90

Bear Backpack 94

Bear Rug 95

Boris Bear 96

Bibliography 112

Index 112

Teddy Bears:
Their Place in History

Teddy bears did not arrive upon the American scene inconspicuously. In fact, their origins involved a president, a political cartoon and a pair of entrepreneurs who knew a good thing when they saw it.

Even as a child, Theodore Roosevelt loved to hunt. By the time he became president in 1901, his passion for the hunt and his prowess with a rifle were well known. On November 14, 1902, Roosevelt went bear hunting in Smedes, Mississippi, with Holt Collier (a guide), a Mr. Parker and a Mr. Foote. Shortly after daybreak, the dogs found a bear's trail. To save the president hours of hard riding through rough country, Collier determined where the bear would most likely exit the woods and suggested that Mr. Foote and the president wait there. As noontime approached and no bear appeared, Foote and Roosevelt abandoned all hope of ever seeing the animal and returned to camp for lunch. Had they remained at their post, they would probably have had a clear shot; the bear burst from the woods at almost the exact spot Holt had predicted.

After running for another mile, the bear—lean, black, weighing 235 pounds—found his path blocked by a water hole. Trapped, he turned on the pursuing dogs, killing one instantly. Just as it raised a paw to maul a second dog, Collier galloped up, jumped from his horse and knocked the bear over with a blow to the head. With a blast on his horn to signal that the bear had been found, Collier roped the dazed bear, tied it to a tree and dispatched a messenger to fetch the president.

When Roosevelt arrived, he was adamant: he would not shoot the bear, nor would he permit anyone else to do so. Instead, he instructed that the animal be put out of its misery. The bear's life was ended with a knife.

The next day, *The Washington Post* ran a story on the hunt, entitled "One Bear Bagged (But It Did Not Fall a Trophy to President's Winchester)." The day after that, the paper carried a cartoon by Clifford Berryman, "Drawing the Line in Mississippi." In it the cartoonist likened the president's refusal to shoot with a political dispute then brewing between Mississippi and Louisiana.

The *Post's* coverage attracted nationwide attention, including that of Morris Michtom, a shopkeeper, and his wife, Rose. Inspired by the story, Rose made two bears out of plush fabric, excelsior stuffing and shoe-button eyes and displayed them in the window of the couple's stationery and novelty shop. Delighted with them, Michtom wrote the president and asked permission to manufacture the stuffed animals and name them "Teddy's Bears." President Roosevelt, who lacked neither a sense of humor

"Drawing the Line in Mississippi" by Clifford Berryman. November 16, 1902. Photo from the Collection of the Library of Congress.

nor a good instinct for publicity, agreed. By 1907 the demand for Teddy's Bears was so great that the Michtoms exchanged their small shop for a large loft, where they founded the Ideal Novelty and Toy Company.

After almost 90 years, teddy bears are still treasured toys. Although we now have an endless variety of fabrics, colors and styles to choose from, each bear remembers its beginnings. And although it may seem ironic that the death of one bear occasioned the birth of the most famous bruin in history, perhaps the simple decency and compassion of that event will keep teddy bears alive forever.

Original 1903 Teddy Bear made by the Ideal Toy Company.
Photo courtesy of the Smithsonian Institution.

Bear
Necessities

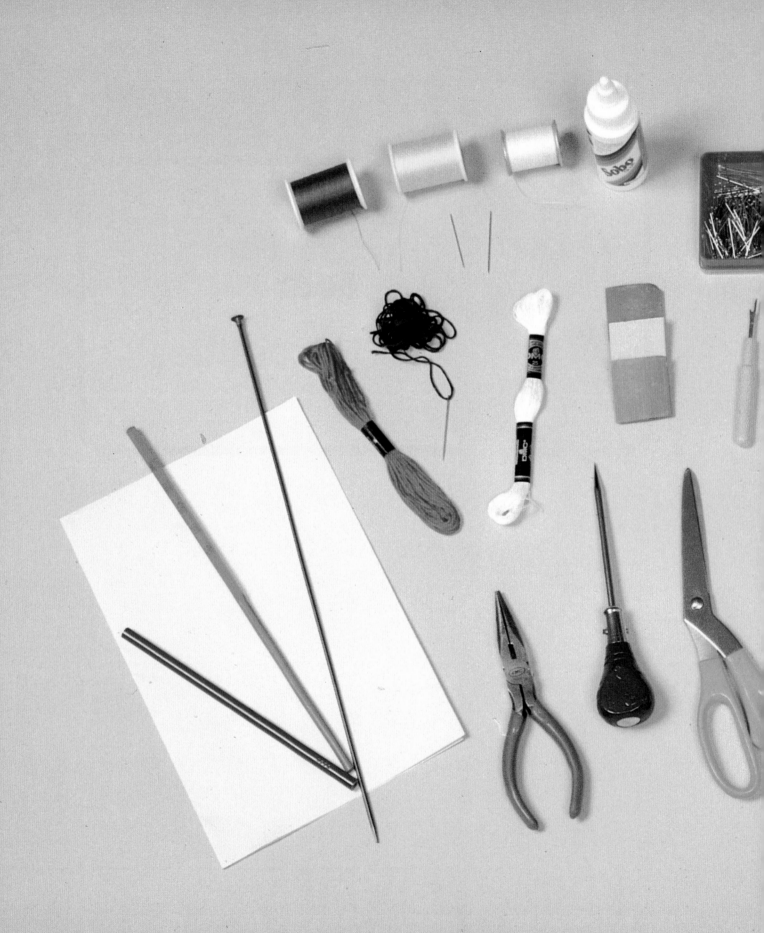

Fabrics

Traditionally, bears were made of mohair or alpaca. Mohair comes from the Angora goat and it has a distinct odor, especially when wet. Modern mohair plush is a blend of wool and cotton, and has no odor. Alpaca comes from the South American alpaca, a relative of the llama. It is denser than mohair and not as expensive. Either mohair or alpaca can be found at an upholstery shop. Alpaca sells for approximately $80-$125 a yard, while mohair can cost from $100 - $130 a yard.

Bears can be made from a great variety of materials. Knits, corduroy, terry cloth, velour, velvet, synthetic suede, denim, calico, or even lace can be used to make a bear. While we have chosen corduroy, terry cloth and felt for our bears, you may prefer to use synthetic fur.

Synthetic fur is a blend of manmade fibers such as nylon, polyester, acrylic, and modacrylic. It is shinier than real fur and mohair, but is inexpensive, durable, and can be found in a wide range of colors, textures, and thicknesses. Synthetic fur is also called fake fur, fur-by-the-yard, or acrylic fur.

Most fake furs have a knit backing that is flexible. Some are stiffer and less likely to be stretched out of shape when stuffed. Check to see just how much the backing will stretch before purchasing. You want it to give some, but you want your bear to maintain a bear's shape and not be stretched out of shape.

It is important that the fur fabric you choose be durable, flame resistant, and washable. If you fold the fabric in half and look at the fur in the fold you can get a good idea of how quickly the fur will show wear and tear. If the fur is thin, it will not wear very long. Look for fur that does not thin out when folded in half. Try to find out what the fabric is made of and how to safely clean it. Always test clean a piece of extra fur before starting to use it for your bear.

As bears vary in size and thickness, so should the fur. Select the correct pile for the bear you will be making. As a rule of thumb, medium bears look nice with a ½" pile fur while large bears look nice with a ¾" pile fur.

Fake fur material tends to slide as you stitch it. You will avoid this problem if you carefully pin the pieces together, with right sides of the fur

Notice the thinning of the fur on the fold in the top piece. The bottom piece is more suitable.

together, and hand baste each piece. An alternative is to place a sheet of tracing paper between the fur pieces before pinning and stitching. The paper is easily torn away after the seam is stitched.

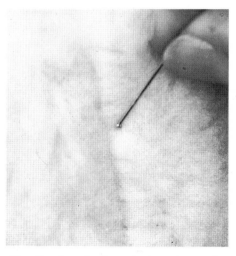

Use the head of a pin to release fur caught in the seam.

The fur may flatten and get caught inside the seam while stitching. Try brushing the fur inward before pinning and stitching, but you'll find that some will inevitably get caught in the seam. The bits that do get caught can be pulled out by running the head of a dressmaker pin over the seam, one side at a time, until the bits come out. This makes the seam less visible and fluffs up the nap.

Nap

Fur fabrics have a definite nap. To determine the direction of the nap, run your hand over the surface. If it feels rough, you are going against the nap; if it feels smooth, you are going with the nap. The nap of fur is a lighter color when stroked downward and a darker color when stroked upward.

The nap of every fabric should be found before any pattern pieces are laid out to be cut. If the pieces are not cut with the nap running in the same direction, they will be unevenly shaded. While this may not be apparent on some pieces, it will be obvious on the bear's head. If the pieces are laid out as shown in the diagram, this will not occur and you will not have to cut another piece later.

The pattern pieces have arrows marked on them to show the nap running in a downward direction. Most bear heads have two side pieces and one center piece and/or a back head piece. This can be confusing when laying out the pieces to be cut. For this reason, every bear project has a suggested layout diagram provided for you. The pieces are arranged in such a way that they will be cut correctly and the nap will be running in the same direction.

If you are a beginner, it is a good idea to purchase more material than required, at least for your first bear project. This way, if you make a mistake, you can easily cut another piece and start over. If you are one of the lucky ones who makes no mistakes, you can use the extra material to make the ears, paw or foot pads, snouts or muzzles for another bear. Or, you can make an extra bear to give as a gift and show off your newfound knowledge.

Remnants

Remnants are leftovers from bolts of fabric that are sold at a reduced price. Remnants can be found in fabric, discount, and department stores. They are available in many types of fabric and even though you may not always find the exact color you want, the price is usually reduced enough to make you take a second look. Regular fur prices range from $9.99 to $15.99 per yard, and the plush fur prices start at $15.99 per yard. But when it becomes a remnant, its price may drop to $6.99 to $10.99 per yard. Remnant sales at your local fabric store may reduce prices even further.

Storing Fabric

When storing contrasting colors of fur in the same bag or box (yellow and brown, for example), turn the colored fur inward as you fold up the material, placing the backings together. This way, the different colors of pile will not stick to one another and you won't have to pick tufts of one color off another.

Cleaning Fur Fabrics

To clean your bear, use a spray bottle filled with a mild detergent and water solution. Before spraying the bear, test the solution on an extra piece of each different color you have used to see if it will damage the material. Alter the solution as needed, either by adding more water or changing the detergent. Vacuum the bear to remove any dirt, dust, or lint in the fur. Lightly mist the bear with the solution. Carefully wipe the bear with a damp cloth, moving the cloth in overlapping circles. You can use a hair dryer to blow the bear dry or let him air dry. After he is dry, you can lightly brush him to fluff up his fur and make him soft and cuddly looking again.

You can also clean your bear with a color-safe carpet cleaner, just as you would clean your carpets. Vacuum first to remove any dust, dirt, or lint. Carefully use a damp brush to work in the carpet cleaner. Let it dry overnight, then vacuum off.

Sewing Techniques

Darts

Fold fabric along center of dart. Beginning at widest part at edge of fabric, stitch to point. Backstitch to knot thread. For fur, slash along center to ½ - 1" (1.2 - 2.5 cm) from the point; press or finger press open.

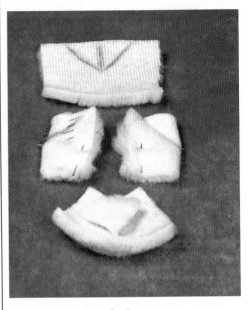

Steps for sewing darts.

Seam Allowances

You will not be required to add a seam allowance to any of the pattern pieces in this book as a ¼" seam allowance has already been added. The inside line shows the ¼" seam allowance and your sewing machine stitching should be on this line when sewing the pieces of your bear together. Most of the pattern pieces are full-sized, so tracing the pattern piece just as it is will be all that you are required to do.

Clipping Seam Allowance

Curved seams will need to be clipped so that they will lie flat. After sewing, clip into the seam about ⅛" (3 mm), at intervals of an inch or so, depending on the tightness of the curve. The seams will then be pressed open or pressed to one side and the edges overcast.

Cutting Out Pattern Pieces

After you have determined the nap direction, lay out the pattern pieces on the wrong side of the material (the wrong side has no fur, only the backing), according to the suggested layout pattern.

The pattern pieces can be traced from the book onto tracing paper or you can photocopy them and pin the copies to your material. If you photocopy the book patterns, however, you may find it difficult to work with the stiff copy paper. If you use tracing paper, simply trace the pattern pieces onto the paper with a pencil or whatever you prefer to work with (several different tracing methods are available at fabric stores).

As you complete each piece, make sure that you label which piece it is and that you mark the nap directions. Mark all pieces with dots for joints, lines for darts, openings for stuffing and turning, dots for eye and nose placement, and ear placements, if any. You would be surprised how easy it is to confuse the pieces when it is time to assemble the bear, so label each piece carefully as you cut it out.

Arrange the pattern pieces on the wrong side of the material and pin. We recommend using dressmakers pins, which are longer than regular pins and work well with thick fur fabrics. Before cutting, you can draw around the pattern pieces with tailor's chalk or magic marker on fur, or a soft pastel pencil on thin fabric. There are several markers on the market that dissolve or fade away. If you do not want to draw around the pattern piece, simply cut around it. Use sharp scissors and cut as close as you can without damaging the pattern piece; chances are you will need to use the same pattern piece again.

Fabrics other than fur can be cut with the material doubled. This is not recommended for fur. Some plush fur can be quite thick and, when doubled, the margin for error is greatly increased; you may cut more of the fur on the bottom layer than you realize. If you need to cut more than one of the same piece, re-pin and cut another one in the same manner.

For pattern pieces that are placed on the fold of the material, you will need to alter the directions when using fur. Pin the piece to the wrong side of the material and cut it out on all sides except the one marked "Fold." Mark the fold line, reverse the piece, and cut out the opposite side. Take care to match up seam lines so that the piece will smoothly progress from side to side.

Some pieces will have to be reversed on the material. To do this, place the pattern piece on the material, pin, and cut out. Then reverse the piece (so that all the writing is facing down into the backing of the material), pin, and cut out. You will need to do this until you have the number of pieces needed. You will have to cut out four of each arm and leg (each arm and leg pattern piece will be cut out twice with right side facing up and twice in reverse or with the writing facing down).

If you are using fur, lightly brush the cut edges of the material (both the piece you cut out and the piece left over) to remove the loose fur and save yourself from picking it up off the floor, table, sewing machine, or wherever else the material has been. If you can cut through the backing only and not the pile of fur, there won't be any loose fur to pick up. However, this is difficult to do.

When buying fur, try to buy the thread at the same time. It is important to get as close a color match as possible, because the ears and stuffing openings are hand-sewn. A well-matched sewing thread will hide the majority of stitching sins.

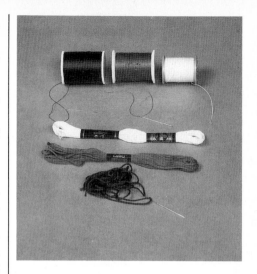

The standard cotton-covered polyester thread is a good choice for strong seams. You can use a thicker sewing machine embroidery thread for appliqué or double strands of regular sewing thread. To anchor button eyes, arms and legs, and head, use a tough nylon or polyester thread. To embroider noses, mouths, or eyes use six-strand cotton embroidery floss or a tightly twisted rayon or silk embroidery floss.

Safety

Most of the eyes recommended in this book are safety eyes. Safety eyes consist of the fronts (the parts that are seen on the outside of the bear) and the childproof locking disk that attaches to the front inside the bear.

Safety eyes and noses.

They come in different sizes and colors. If a bear pattern calls for a glass eye and you do not feel comfortable with glass eyes around your small child, just substitute any eyes you prefer or feel safe with. If you have concerns about button eyes coming off or glass eyes breaking and injuring your child, consider satin stitching the eyes on your bear. Felt can also be used in many colors and shapes.

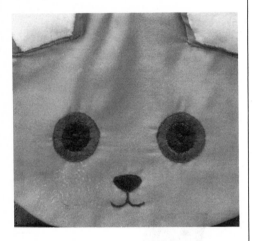

Sample of satin stitched eyes and nose.

Plastic noses are recommended in this book. They have a front piece that is seen on the outside of the head, with a locking disk attached inside the bear. You may substitute stitching or felt for the nose if you have safety concerns about the plastic parts.

Labelling Each Bear

If you know you will be making more than one of the same bear, it is a good idea to label each piece with the name of the bear on it (or a number assigned to each bear). You can keep the bears separate this way and not worry about a stray pattern piece making its way onto the wrong bear. It is also a good idea to keep each bear's instructions and pattern pieces in an individual manilla envelope. This way, when you get ready to make another bear, everything will be in the same place, organized and ready.

Stitches Used

Embroidery Stitches

Stem Stitch: Work from left to right, taking regular, slightly slanted stitches along the line of the design. The thread always emerges on the left side of the previous stitch.

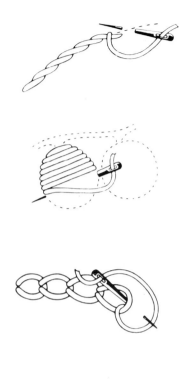

Satin Stitch: Work straight stitches across the shape desired. Do not make the stitches too long, as they might be pulled out of position.

Chain Stitch: Bring the thread out at top of line and hold down with left thumb. Insert the needle where it last emerged and bring the point out a short distance away. Pull the thread through, keeping the working thread under the needle point.

Back Stitch: Bring the thread through on the stitch line, then take a small backward stitch through the fabric. Bring the needle through again a little in front of the first stitch, then take another backward stitch, pushing the needle in at the point where it first came through.

Other Stitches

Whip Stitch: Place the folded back bottom edge over the front bottom edge. Bring needle up at A. Insert needle down through B and out at C, down through D and out at E, etc.

Handbasting Stitch: Pin specified edges together. Bring a needle in and out of the fabric along the stitching lines making ⅛" stitches ⅛" apart.

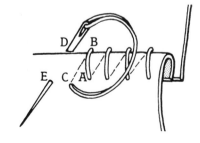

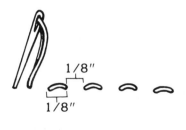

Individual
Piece
Construction

Legs and Arms

In order to shape the legs and arms correctly, each pattern piece must be reversed and cut out again. This means that for each arm there will be one piece cut just as the pattern piece shows and one piece cut with the pattern piece reversed. The same applies to the legs.

After sewing side and top of leg seam, leaving an opening for turning, sew in the sole pieces.

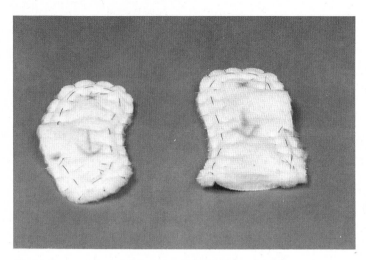

Baste the arm and leg seams before sewing.

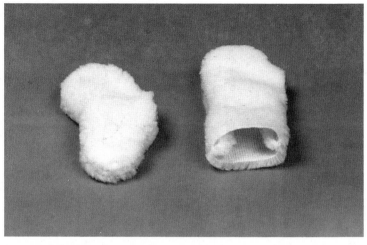

Turn the arm and leg pieces right side out.

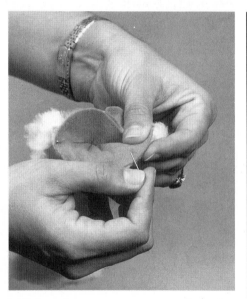

After sewing leg seam, sew the sole piece into bottom of leg.

Note: Only the inside arm or leg pieces (the side closest to the body) will have a hole punched in them to insert the joints. The opening left for stuffing and turning can be left anywhere, but it is easier to stitch a straight line than a curved one.

Openings for turning and stuffing in the leg pieces.

Head

Bear heads are confusing at first. There are several pieces that make up the head. Each bear has different pieces, but all have two sides of the head (except Max) that are sewn into a center piece and/or a snout or muzzle.

Unless specified in the directions, all side head pieces have to have one side piece reversed before cutting to achieve the correct shaping. The center piece lays between both side head pieces and the eyes are usually placed on the center piece or in the seams connecting the side to the center piece.

When pinning the side head piece to the center head piece, it is a good idea to pin, baste, and then sew one side first. Then pin, baste and sew the other side. This way, you will not have as much material to keep out of your way and the pins from both sides will not be poking you as you are stitching.

Remove the hand basting after sewing head pieces together.

Pieces making up the head of the bear.

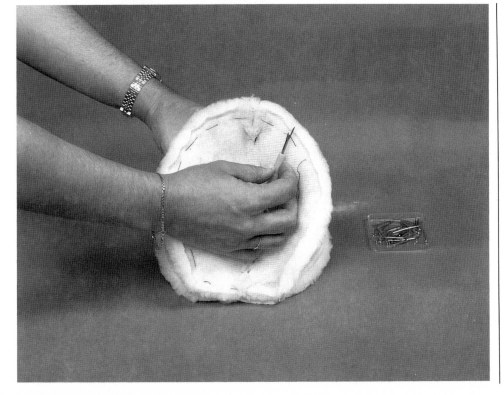

The center head piece can run the entire middle of the head or only to the nose, to be met by another piece called a snout or muzzle.

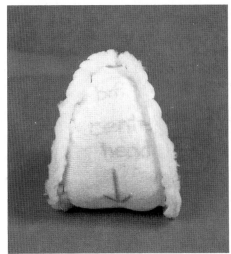

Position center head piece to side head pieces and sew.

19

The snout or muzzle is added to the head piece to give the bear additional shaping. If there is an upper and lower snout, the upper snout extends from the top of the head to the nose and the lower snout extends from the nose down to the neck.

After sewing the center seams of the snout or muzzle, attach the plastic nose where indicated on the pattern (or where you prefer).

Sew center seams of snout. Turn snout right side out.

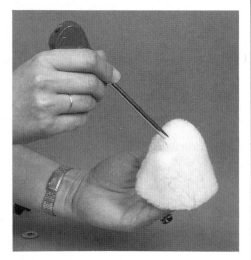

Make hole for plastic nose with an awl.

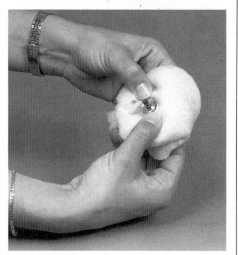

Attach the locking disk firmly onto the back of the plastic nose.

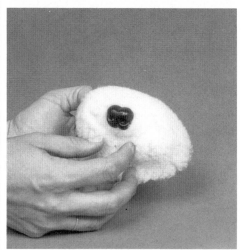

Turn snout right side out.

You will have to make a hole for the nose with the awl. Push the plastic nose through the hole and attach the locking disk firmly onto the back of nose, inside the head.

After attaching nose, sew snout onto head by hand.

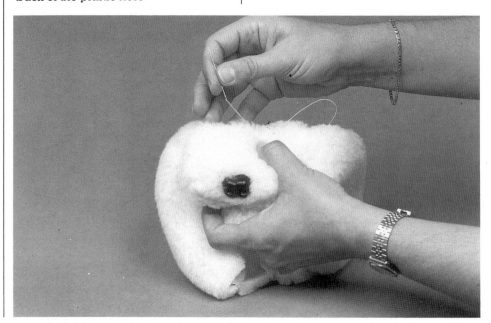

Eyes

The hole for the eyes is made with an awl (or ice pick). Push the awl through the material where indicated (or where you think best). Using your ruler, measure to make sure the other eye hole is the correct distance and height from the first eye hole. The eyes are pushed through the hole in the material and the locking disk firmly attached into the back of the eye, inside the head.

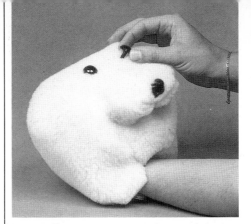

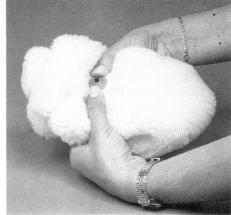

Set eyes in place and secure with locking disk inside of head.

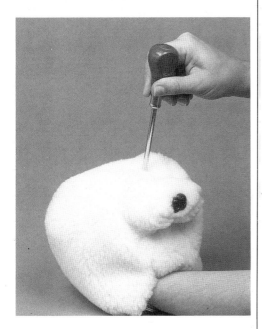

Punch hole with awl for eye placement. Measure placement for second eye.

Various positions of the eyes result in different expressions for the bears.

Ears

With right sides together (fur facing fur), pin ears together, leaving the lower edge open for turning and stuffing. Sew ear pieces together, then turn right side out. (It is advisable to baste them first to keep the fur from shifting.)

If a contrasting color is to be used for the ear front, sew contrasting color to ear front before sewing front to back ear.

Ear piece that has been sewn and turned.

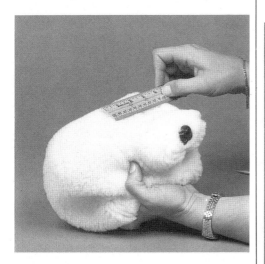

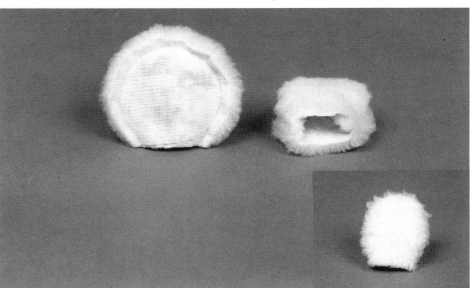

You can hand-sew the ears directly to the top of head where indicated on pattern pieces or, when darts are called for, place the ear in the dart before sewing and machine-stitch the ear directly into the dart.

Above: Finished head piece.
Left: Pin ears in place and sew by hand.

Various positions of the ears result in different expressions for the bears.

Note: Ears are tricky. Placement may have to be adjusted before sewing the ears on. While it is easier to sew the ears on before stuffing, the entire head shape is best seen after stuffing. Any mistakes can then be easily detected and the ears adjusted to fit accordingly. While it may not be crucial for the head to be exact, the ears will be very obvious if slightly off balance. Try pinning the ears on before sewing, and if they need adjusting after the head is stuffed, simply unpin and reposition.

The head can be attached to the bear two different ways. You can sew all the pieces to the head, turn right side out and stuff, and then hand stitch head to neck. Or you can finish the head, leaving fur inside out, machine stitch head to neck, and then turn right side out. The head can be stuffed when the rest of the bear is stuffed through the opening in the neck. Any hard to reach places in the head can be reached with the use of a chopstick, knitting needle, or pencil. If using a sharp pointed tool, be careful not to stick it through the fur while moving the stuffing around.

Body

The bear bodies come in differing pattern pieces. Usually, the front bear body will be in two different pieces, making it larger than the back and allowing more stuffing to be inserted to round out the belly. The bear back may be in one or two pieces. When two back pieces are called for, one of these will have to be reversed to assure correct shaping. Make sure that you stitch the front to the back with each side matching up evenly. The obvious overlapping of the bear front will fill up after stuffing.

Holes will need to be punched with the awl for the bear arms and legs to be inserted with joints. Push the awl through the dot drawn on the pattern pieces. You will need four holes: two for the arms, two for the legs.

An opening should be left for stuffing. Although you can leave an opening almost anywhere, it is much easier to stitch a straight line than a curved one, so we have called for the opening to be left where it is on a straight line and easiest to hide the stitches. You can place special options inside the body, such as a music box, growler, or squeaker. See Options section for further details.

Pin and baste body pieces before sewing.

Joints

For joints to connect the arms and legs to the body, you can use buttons, cotter pins with disks, or plastic joints.

Buttons are a traditional and easy method for joining bears together. To use buttons for joints, you will need a long (five- to eight-inch) doll-making needle and heavy duty thread. (If you use elastic thread, it will break easily when pulled.) You will sew from one side of the bear to the other to hold the arms and legs firmly in place.

Insert the needle into the arm, through the body, out the other side of the body, the other arm, and then back and forth until you get the tension just the way you want the arms to be when finished. Use the same method for the legs. Adjust the arms and legs to get them as loose or as tight as you would like them.

The buttons can be decorative, like those on the Sweetheart Bear, and remain on the outside of the arms and legs, or they can be plain buttons concealed on the inside of the arms and legs, with stuffing around them.

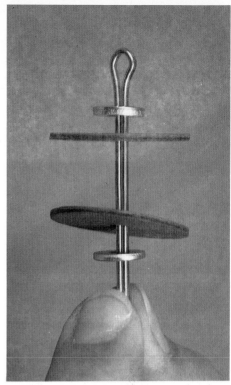

Pieces making up cotter pin set.

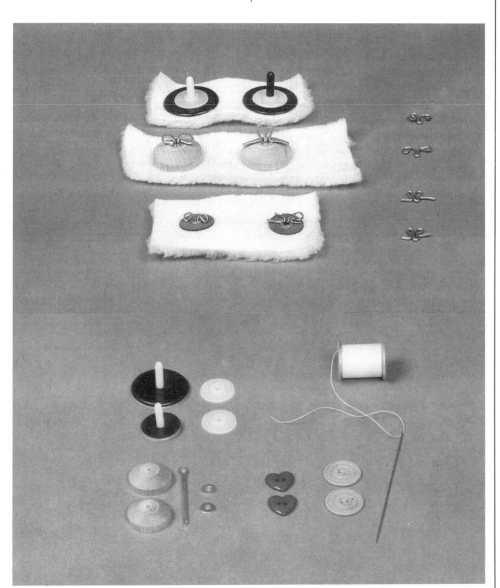

Various materials used for joint constructions.

The cotter pin (or key) is used with hardboard disks and washers. Use the awl to punch holes into the inside (the part touching the bear body) arm and leg for the cotter pin to fit through. You will also need needle nose (or long nose) pliers to bend the ends of the pin to firmly hold the arms and legs to the body.

The cotter pin is pushed through the washer and hardboard disk, through the hole in the arm and the hole in the body side (where marked on your pattern pieces with a dot). While in the body, add the other hardboard disk and washer to the cotter pin. Now you are ready to bend the pin to hold the arm to the body. Bending the cotter pin takes practice. Before using any cotter pins in your bear, first experiment bending them outside of the bear, with either a test piece of fur or just the hardboard disks together. Buy several extra cotter pins to practice with. After you have the feel and tension of the pin, go on to the bear.

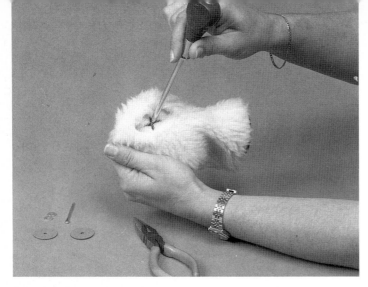

Punch hole in arm and leg pieces with awl for cotter pin.

Insert cotter pin from inside to outside of arm and leg pieces.

Make sure all holes have been punched into the bear body. There should be two for the arms and two for the legs. Punch one hole in each side of the arms and legs where they will be joined to the body.

Push the pin through one hardboard disk and washer, insert into the arm and push through to the inside of the bear body. Add one more hardboard disk and washer, then grab with the needle nose pliers. Either bend the ends into a circle or a bow, whichever you feel most comfortable with. Adjust the tension on the pin until you get the degree of movement you want for the arm. Don't leave the pin loose or it will not hold at all. Repeat the steps

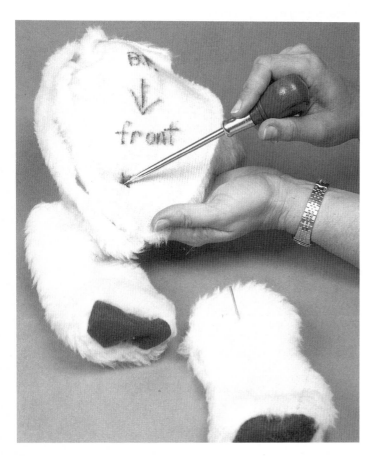

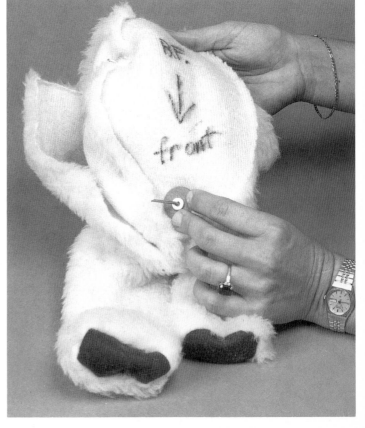

Punch holes in body to insert cotter pins.

Insert cotter pins in arm and leg prior to inserting pieces into body.

until all the arms and legs have been attached.

Note: You could insert the pin from the body to the arm, but you would have less room to work in (the arm is smaller than the body) and there would be less stuffing around the pin in the arm than there would be in the body, thereby increasing the possibility of injury to a child falling on the arm or leg.

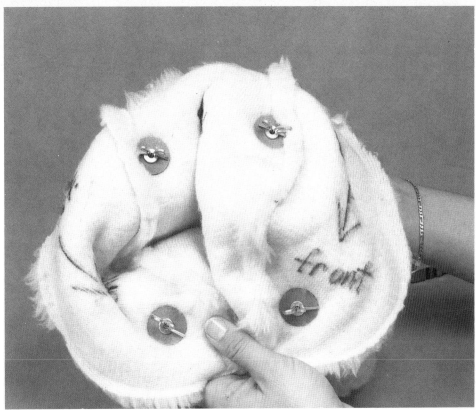

Inside of body after assembling cotter pin joints.

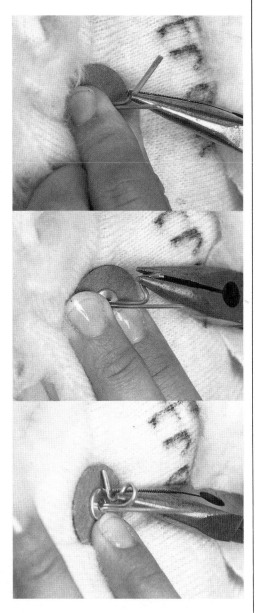

Steps for tightening cotter pins.

The cotter pins and washers can be found at any hardware store. The hardboard disks are another story. They can be found by calling hobby stores, craft shops, or fabric stores, but most likely by locating a doll-making shop (dolls use joints also). If you have exhausted every local source, use one of the mail-order suppliers we have listed on page 110. While waiting for your supplies to arrive, you can make the bear up to the jointing stage.

If you would rather not have button or cotter pin joints, plastic joints are now available. They are easier to find and less expensive than the hardboard disks, and are either pushed or screwed together (similar to the eyes and noses). They have only three parts to them: one disk with a shaft, one disk with a center hole, and the locking disk. Insert the disk with the shaft first. Push the shaft through the arm into the body and insert disk with hole in center. Push locking disk firmly onto shaft to secure. The hole you insert them through has to be larger than the hole used for the cotter pin.

Stuffing

For the bears in this book, polyester fiber was chosen as the stuffing material. You can choose alternatives such as excelsior, kapok, cotton batting, or old material scraps or rags you have left over.

Polyester stuffing.

Excelsior was traditionally used in bear making. It is made from the shavings of wood and is messy to work with, flammable, and not washable. (It also comes in a paper version.) Because it makes a firm shape when stuffed into a bear, many old bears stuffed with excelsior are still around some 80 years later. Excelsior should only be used for a collector's bear, not for a child's bear. Excelsior can be found in a hardware store or at a taxidermy shop.

Kapok was once commonly used to stuff bears. It is made from the fiber covering the seeds of the Ceiba tree. It is very expensive and hard to obtain. Most kapok is imported from England. It is heavier than other stuffings and bits of it will float in the air while you are using it, but it has a silky texture and does not produce lumps.

Cotton batting is commonly used in quiltmaking. It is easy to find and inexpensive, but more expensive than polyester fiber. It is washable but dries slowly. When used for stuffing, pull it apart so it is an even consistency and does not produce lumps.

Polyester fiber is the most commonly used stuffing material. It is lightweight, easy to work with, washable, durable, inexpensive, and can be found from department stores to fabric stores. It comes in a variety of qualities, so choose the one you want your bear to feel like. If you watch the stores, you can even find it on sale periodically.

When stuffing with polyester fiber, pull it apart and stuff by the handful into the bear. To help you fill the small, tight areas of the bear, use a dowel stick, knitting needle, chopstick, or pencil. Keep in mind that you do not want to damage the fur in any way while using one of these tools to maneuver the stuffing around. The chopstick or an unsharpened pencil has dull ends that will not poke through the fur while using.

As you stuff the bear, massage the stuffing into the desired shape. After stuffing, pin the opening shut and check the look and feel of each piece. Some mistakes are obvious only after the stuffing has been added. By pinning first, you can easily restuff any section before the final stitches sew the openings together.

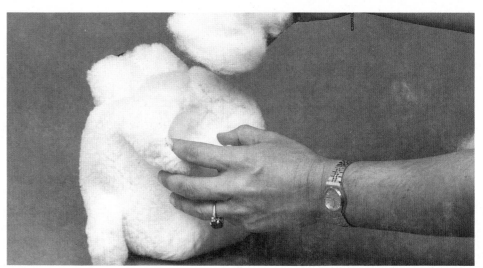

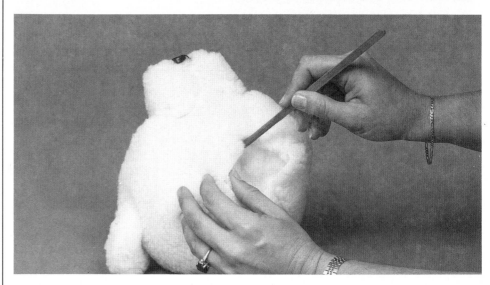

Stuffing procedure.

Options

There are options that you can add to your bears, to make them even more special. You can add a music box, growler box, a squeaker, or a pull-string talking unit. These are not found everywhere and you may have to order from one of the following suppliers:

A Stitch in Time, 1259 Sweeten Creek Road, Asheville, NC 28803 (eyes, nose, joints, squeakers)

Merrily Doll Supply Co., 8542 Ranchito Avenue, Panorama City, CA 91402 (catalog of supplies, including pull-string talking unit)

by Diane, 1126 Ivon Ave., Endicott, NY 13760 (German growlers, eyes, noses, joint sets, materials including mohair and alpaca. Catalog $1.75.)

Options are added to the bear after the body has been stuffed to the stomach and you have sewn the opening halfway up. Be sure to leave enough space for the option you've chosen.

Music Box

The music box is inserted into the bear's back. It has a winding key that unscrews from the shank that inserts into the metal case. Unscrew the key and set aside. In order to hold the music box firmly in position and keep any stuffing from entering, you will need to cover the music box before inserting it into the bear. You can use cheesecloth, net, voile, or organdy wide enough to go around the box and whipstitch the ends together. Gather and stitch both ends together. Push the shank of the music box through the fabric covering.

Insert the box so the end with the shank sticking out is facing the inside of the bear. Try to position it as close to the center of the bear's back as possible. With the awl, make a hole in the bear fur for the shank. Screw the key onto the shank so that it will not slip back through the bear's back. Sew the covered music box to the inside of the bear's back with heavy duty thread. Don't let the stitches show on the outside of the bear's back. Pack the rest of stuffing around the box to keep it in place.

Growlers and Squeakers

Both the growler and the squeaker have cylinder shapes with holes in one end. When tipped, a weight presses on a bellows forcing air past a reed, making a big bear growl or a small bear squeak. Both growlers and squeakers are inserted into the bear's front.

The squeaker can be covered with a piece of cheesecloth, net, voile, or organdy. It can then be sewn into the bear's belly so that every time the bear is hugged it will squeak. You might prefer some other place for inserting the squeaker.

The growler can also be covered with a piece of cheesecloth, net, voile, or organdy. Insert the growler in the bear's stomach, making sure that the end covered with holes faces toward the front of the bear. Sew the growler to the bear's belly with heavy duty thread. If the round outline of the growler is visible through the bear's fur, place a layer of stuffing in front of it, but not so much that it will muffle the sound.

Bear Friends

Cuddly Bear

Cuddly Bear loves rocking chairs. He can sit and rock and look out the window all day long. He'd much rather sit in your lap, though, and let you do the rocking, as his feet don't quite touch the floor. See page 38.

Olaf and Ollie

Olaf and Ollie are special friends. They never have to be lonely because they are always together. They're very agreeable guys and would be welcome additions to any family. *See page 42.*

Sweetheart Bear

Sweetheart Bear loves to be read to. She cries at the love stories and isn't all that good at solving mysteries, but she enjoys them all just the same. She also likes it when you tell her one of your own stories. See page 50.

Panda Bear

Panda Bear is a born dancer. If left alone, he will almost certainly turn up the music and have a party. Don't be surprised if he invites all the neighbors and they dance until dawn. See page 62.

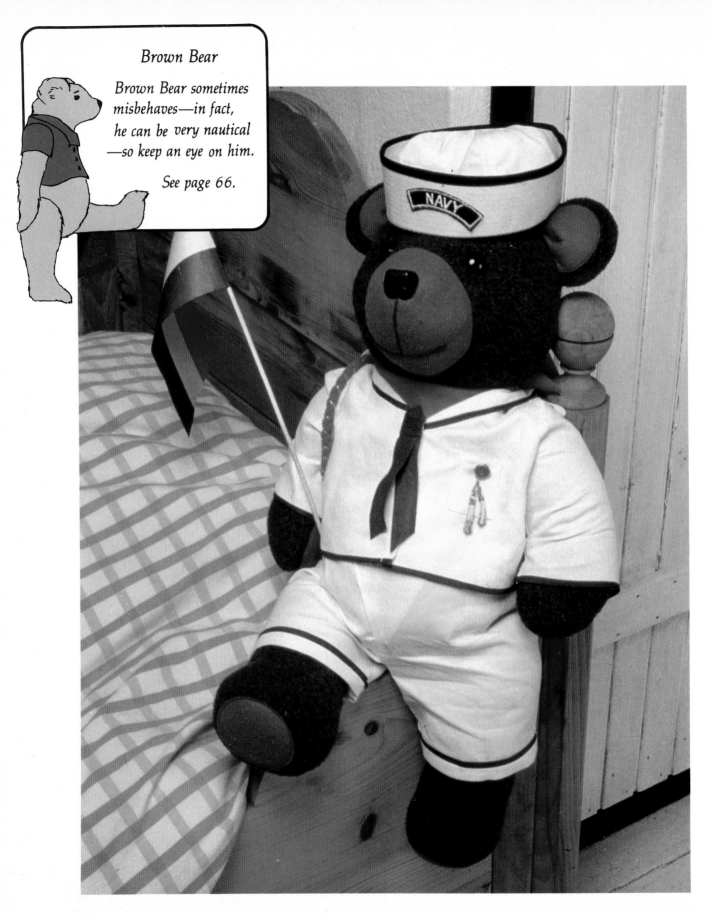

Brown Bear

Brown Bear sometimes misbehaves—in fact, he can be very nautical —so keep an eye on him.

See page 66.

Petie Polar Bear

Petie is a bit of a mischievous chap. He's an adventurer and daredevil wrapped into one bear. A daring child will love his spirit and spunk. See page 76.

Max loves the outdoors. He especially enjoys bike riding and sports. Any day that the weather is nice, you're sure to find Max on the playground with the other kids, cheering on the home team.

MAX BEAR

Size
App. 8½" tall.

Materials
2 pieces of yellow felt, small amounts of felt in colors shown in photo. Embroider thread in various colors. Fiberfill. Bias seam binding.

Directions
Trace the pattern pieces on tissue paper twice. Use 1 sheet of tissue paper for cutting the major body piece and 1 as a guide for the decoration. Cut this 2nd paper into sections of color as indicated on sketch. From the yellow felt, cut 2 bear shapes with a ¼" seam allowance all around. From the other pieces of felt, cut small pieces as indicated on sketch without a seam allowance. Cut a piece of seam binding to fit around the outer edges of the bear and pin to edges of back. Zigzag stitch the small pieces of felt to the front of the bear using matching color thread. With brown thread, embroider around the eyes. With white thread, make highlights on the pupils and nose. Embroider the mouth with red thread. Embroider white stripes and the name on the front of the shirt. Outline the sleeve borders in blue and the back of the ears in brown.

Place the back and front with right sides together with seam binding on the outside. Sew around edges, leaving an opening to turn. Turn right side out. Stuff and sew opening closed.

1 = Gold
2 = Brown
3 = Rose
4 = White
5 = Red
6 = Dark Blue
7 = Black

CUDDLY BEAR

Size
App. 13" tall.

Materials
½ yard of fur or fleece material. 2 glass eyes; purchased nose; polyester stuffing; red or black embroidery thread for mouth, ribbon 24" long, tissue or tracing paper.

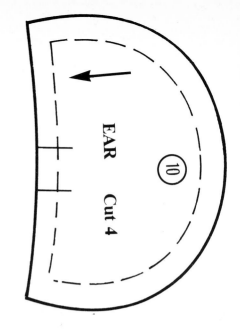

EAR Cut 4

(10)

Directions

Trace the pattern pieces on tracing paper, then pin the tracing paper to the wrong side of fabric as shown on suggested layout diagram. Make sure all pieces follow the arrows drawn on them, with the nap in a downward position. Sew all pieces with right sides together.

Cut 2 pieces of each of the following: the front of the head, the back of the head, front top of foot, bottom of foot and arms. Cut 1 piece each for the following: the muzzle, the back, back legs, back of head, and the front. Cut 4 pieces for the ears.

Head

Mark and sew darts on the front and back head pieces. Sew the center seam of the front of head. Sew the muzzle to front of head then close muzzle center seam. Put in your eyes and nose. Make ears, turn and stuff. Pin in place, remembering the

ears have a fold over pleat. Sew your head front and back pieces together.

Body

Sew your arm seams together, turn and stuff. Sew your foot pieces to the front and back foot pieces to back of legs as indicated. Make a dart in the back seam at neck leaving an opening for stuffing. Sew bottom to back of legs. Sew arms to the front like you did the ears. Sew side seam front and back together by catching the arms in seam. The body can now be connected to the head.

Finishing

Turning head in right direction, insert wrong side out in body and sew around neck, turn bear and finish stuffing. Close bear with whipstitch that will be strong, fluff fur back out with the tip of a needle. Add red or black mouth.

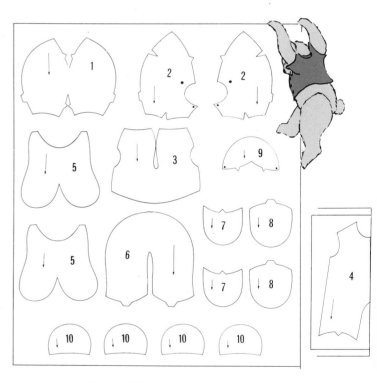

1. Back of Head
2. Front of Head
3. Body Back
4. Body Front and Legs
5. Arm
6. Back Legs and Bottom of Bear
7. Top of Foot
8. Bottom of Foot
9. Muzzle
10. Ear

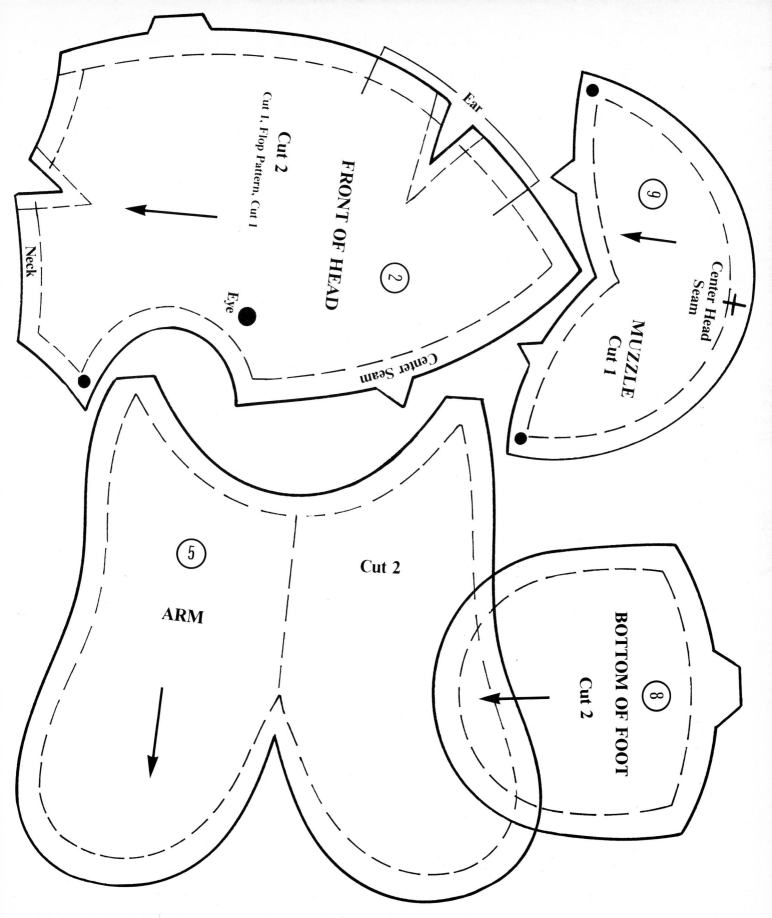

Cut 2
Cut 1, Flop Pattern, Cut 1

FRONT OF HEAD
②

Ear

Neck

Eye

Center Seam

⑨
Center Head Seam

MUZZLE
Cut 1

⑤

Cut 2

ARM

BOTTOM OF FOOT
Cut 2
⑧

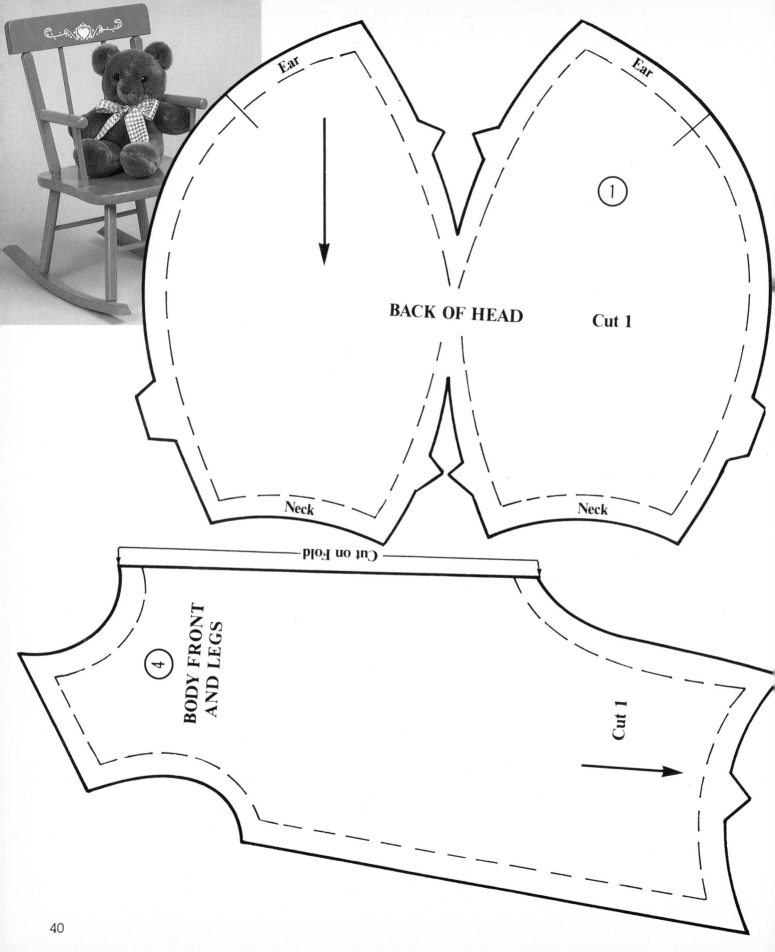

Ear

Ear

①

BACK OF HEAD   Cut 1

Neck

Neck

Cut on Fold

④ **BODY FRONT AND LEGS**

Cut 1

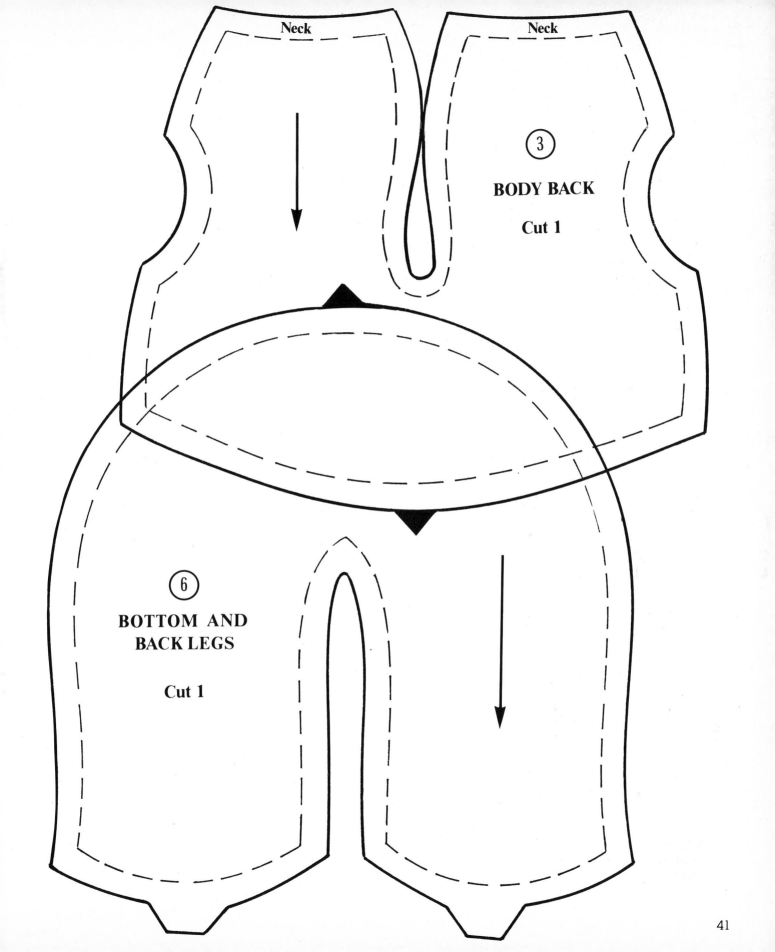

Neck

Neck

③

BODY BACK

Cut 1

⑥

BOTTOM AND BACK LEGS

Cut 1

41

OLAF and OLLIE

Size
Olaf: app. 16½" tall
Ollie: app. 8¼" tall.

Materials
½ yard white fleece, 60" wide; black and blue embroidery floss; 2 purchased blue eyes (or round buttons for eyes); heavy duty thread; 8 large buttons with 2 holes; 8" long needle; polyester stuffing; tissue or tracing paper.

Directions - Olaf

Trace pattern pieces on tracing paper. Then pin to wrong side of fabric, as shown on suggested layout diagram. Make sure all pieces follow the arrows drawn on them, with the nap in a downward position. On doubled fabric, right sides together, cut 2 pieces of front and back of the body and 2 pieces of the side of the head. Cut 4 pieces of both the arms and legs so that 2 pieces are reversed. Cut 1 of the center front piece, cut 2 soles and 4 ears. Sew all pieces with right sides together.

Sew the center front seam of the front of the body. Mark and sew the darts on the sides of the head pieces. Sew neck edge of sides of head to front of body. Sew the side of the head pieces to the upper edges of the back of body as indicated on pattern pieces. Mark position of the nose on center piece between sides of head

pieces and sew seams along sides of head and back pieces. Sew remaining back seam. Sew the side seams of the body. Sew leg inseams. Sew the soles to the bottom of the legs, first basting in place. Turn body and head right side out. Sew eyes on center head piece seams about 2¾" from the nose. With right sides together, sew arms together, leaving straight side open. Mark position of joints. Turn right side out. Stuff.

Finishing
Thread a piece of white sewing thread through 1 hole of a button, then the other hole of button and slide the button to the middle of the thread. Thread both ends of the thread through the needle. Place the button on inside of one arm and sew back and forth through the fabric of the arm and the body at indicated places, then sew through holes of a

second button placed inside body. Continue to sew through buttons of arm and body until firmly joined. Finish stuffing the arm and sew seam. Work same on second arm. Sew neck seam. Embroider

the nose with black thread in satin stitch and the mouth in chain stitch. With right sides together, sew around edges of ears, leaving lower edge open.

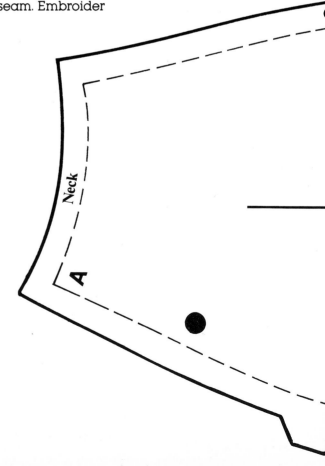

42

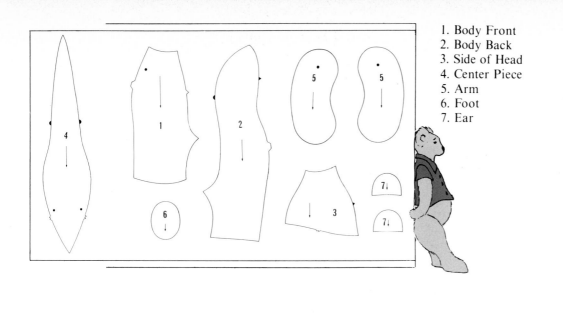

1. Body Front
2. Body Back
3. Side of Head
4. Center Piece
5. Arm
6. Foot
7. Ear

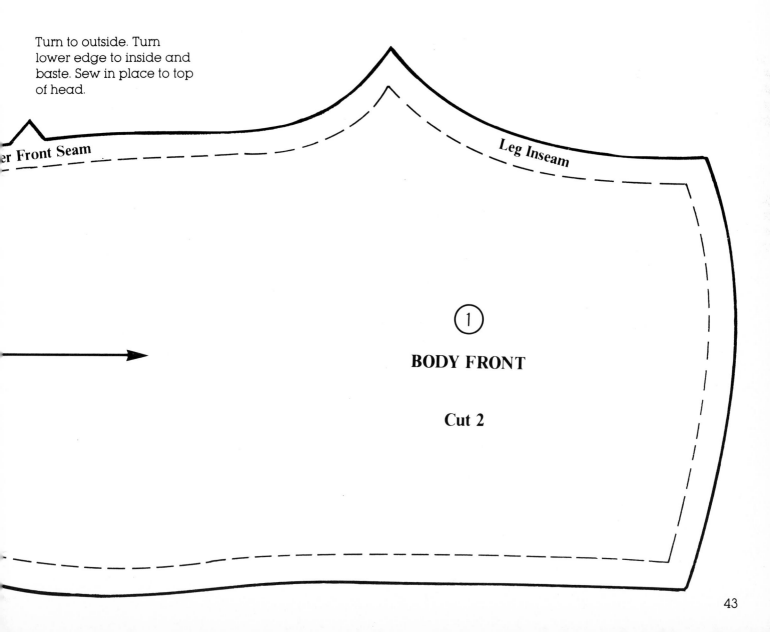

Turn to outside. Turn lower edge to inside and baste. Sew in place to top of head.

er Front Seam

Leg Inseam

①

BODY FRONT

Cut 2

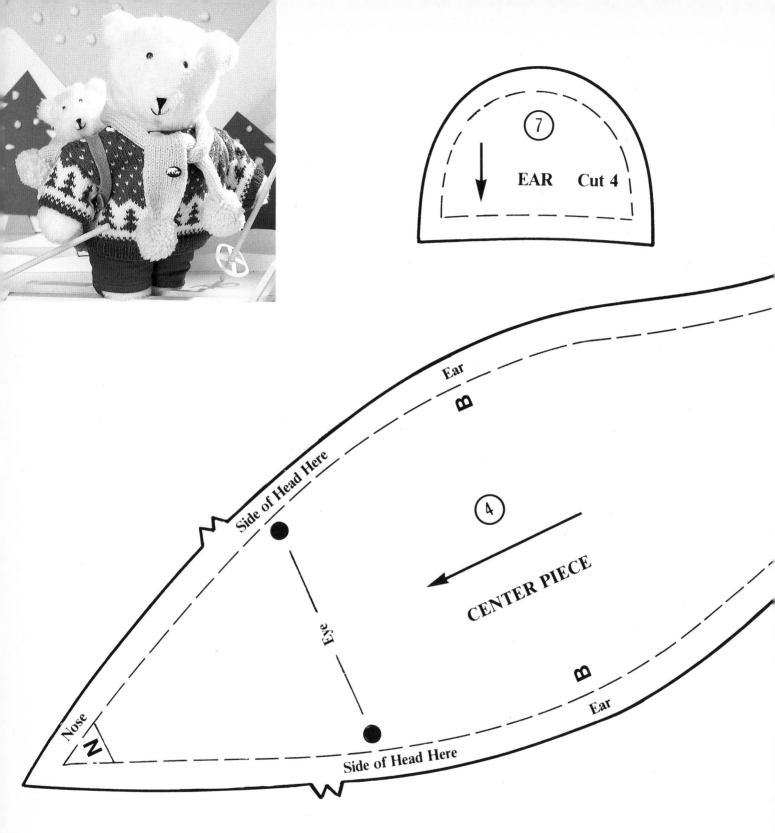

⑦

EAR   Cut 4

Ear

B

Side of Head Here

④

⟵ **CENTER PIECE**

Eye

B

Ear

Nose

N

Side of Head Here

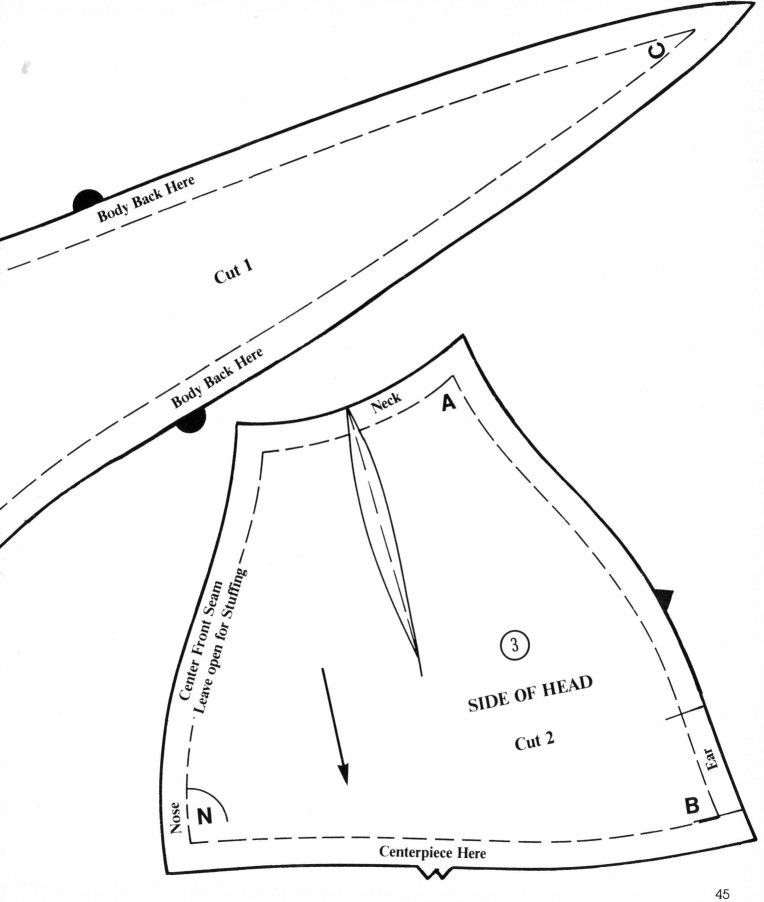

Body Back Here

Cut 1

C

Body Back Here

Neck

A

Center Front Seam
Leave open for Stuffing

③

SIDE OF HEAD

Cut 2

Nose

N

Ear

B

Centerpiece Here

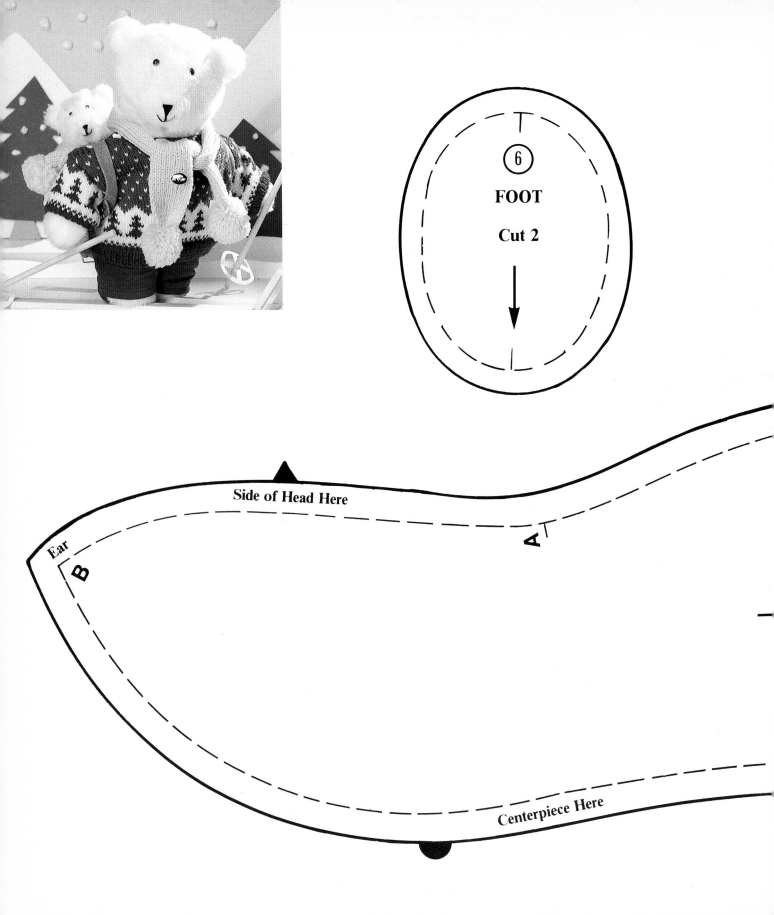

6 FOOT Cut 2

Side of Head Here

Ear

B

A

Centerpiece Here

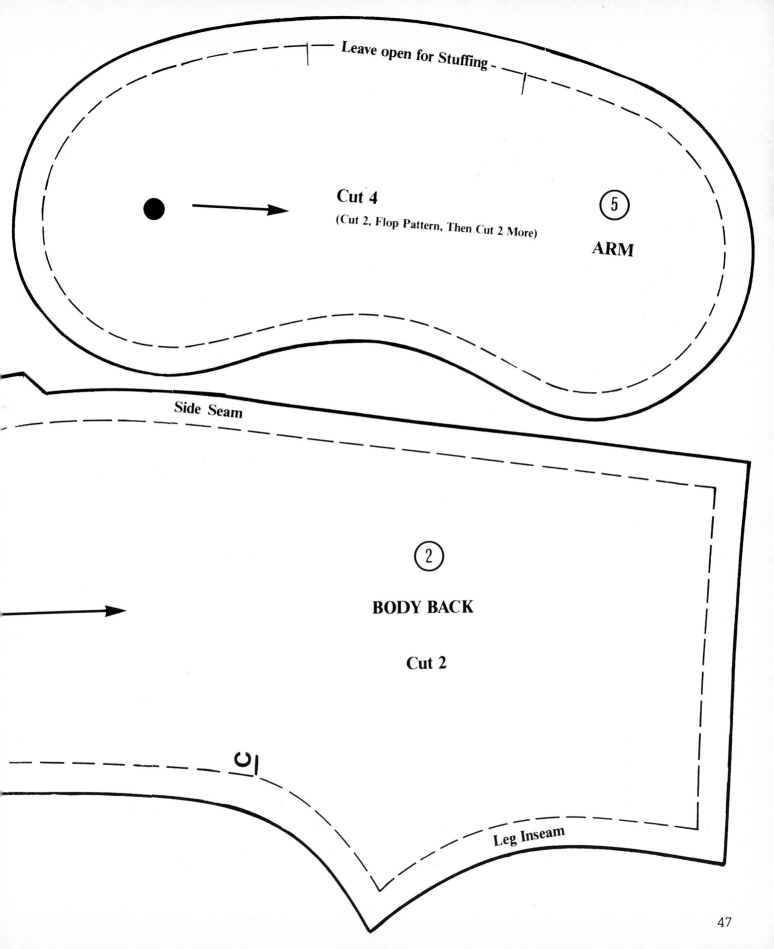

Leave open for Stuffing

Cut 4

(Cut 2, Flop Pattern, Then Cut 2 More)

⑤

ARM

Side Seam

②

BODY BACK

Cut 2

Leg Inseam

47

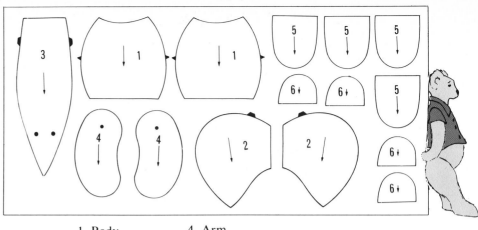

1. Body   4. Arm
2. Side of Head   5. Leg
3. Center Piece   6. Ear

Directions — Ollie

Trace pattern pieces on tracing paper. Then pin the tracing paper to the wrong side of fabric, as shown on suggested layout diagram. Make sure all pieces follow the arrows drawn on them, with the nap in a downward position. On fabric, cut 2 sides of head so that the pieces have reversed shaping, cut 4 arms and legs so that 2 pieces have reversed shaping. Cut 2 pieces for body, 1 piece for center of head, and 4 ears.

With right sides together, sew around edges of legs, leaving straight side open. Turn right side out. Sew to lower edge of front of body, stretching to fit. Sew the side seams of the body. Turn the body right side out. Sew the top of the back of the legs to the lower edge of the back of body. Stuff the legs and close seam by hand.

With right sides together, sew arms, leaving straight side open. Turn right side out and stuff half full.

Thread a piece of white sewing thread through 1 hole of a button, then the other hole of button and slide the button to the middle of the thread. Thread both ends of the thread through the needle. Place the button on inside of one arm and sew back and forth through the fabric of the arm and the body at indicated places, then sew through holes of a second button placed inside body. Continue to sew through buttons of arm and body until firmly joined. Finish stuffing the arm and sew seam. Work same on second arm.

Sew the sides of the head to the center of head with the nose end at the top of center seam of the head. Sew the chin seam. Turn head right side out. With right sides together, sew ears, leaving lower edge open. Turn to outside. Turn lower edges to inside and baste. Sew ears to top of head with top edge at center of head seams. Sew body to

head then stuff. With blue thread, embroider eyes in satin stitch. With black thread, embroider the nose in satin stitch and the mouth in stem stitch.

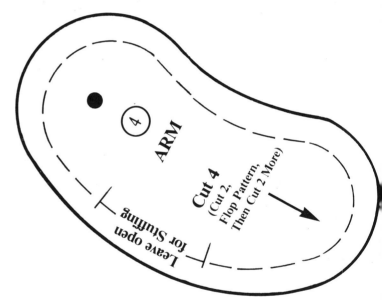

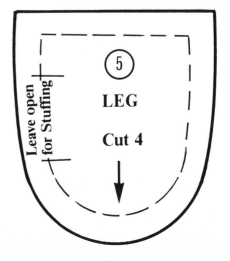

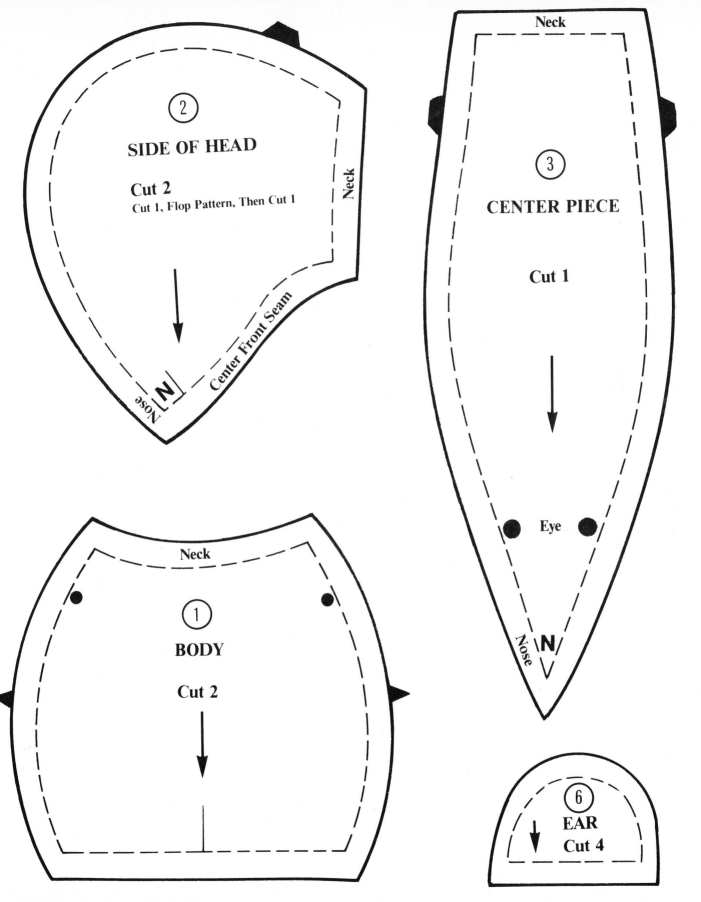

2

SIDE OF HEAD

Cut 2
Cut 1, Flop Pattern, Then Cut 1

Neck

Center Front Seam

Nose

N

3

CENTER PIECE

Cut 1

Neck

Eye

Nose

N

1

BODY

Cut 2

Neck

6

EAR
Cut 4

49

SWEETHEART BEAR

Size
App. 14" tall.

Materials
½ yard white terry cloth, 45" wide. 4" x 4" white felt. Red embroidery thread. 4 red heart buttons ¾" to ⅞" with two or four holes. Purchased eyes and nose. One large bag of polyester stuffing. One spool of red heavy duty thread. One 5" - 8" doll-making needle.

Directions

Trace the pattern pieces on tracing paper. Cut out pattern and lay it to the wrong side of the doubled terry cloth as shown on suggested layout digram. Make sure all pieces follow the arrows drawn on them, with the nap in a downward position. From the terry cloth cut one snout. Double the terry cloth and cut two each: two backs, two fronts, and two sides of the head. From the felt cut two paw pads. Cut four each: four legs, four arms, and four paw pads.

Ears
Sew ears together and turn, sew down dart.

Arms and Legs
Sew paw pad to arm before joining the side seams. Sew pieces right side together leaving an opening on the straight side, turn and stuff. You can close by hand. Make all arms and legs. Topstitch paw pads with contrasting thread.

Head
Sew snout to side head pieces, notch for ears. Sew in ears. Put eyes in place and anchor. Leaving a small opening for nose, close mouth and chin. Put your nose in place and anchor.

Body
Sew center seams together. Sew back seam leaving an opening for turning. Put head and body together and sew neck. Turn and stuff. Close by hand. Attach the arms and legs by using heavy duty thread and your buttons with the long needle. Make an in and out motion through the arm, body, other arm and back. Anchor the arms to where they are firm. Be sure to tie the thread off by wrapping around a button several times and tie. Repeat this step with the legs.

Mouth
Embroider the mouth. Remember you can make your bear happy or sad by the way you shape his mouth. Add a red satin ribbon with a big bow around the neck for a finished look. You can sew a small heart on left side of bear's chest for decoration.

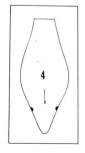

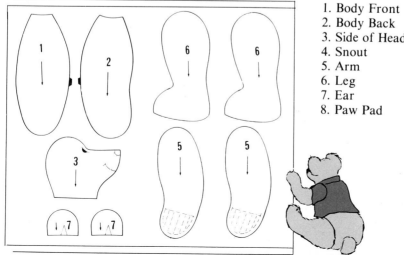

1. Body Front
2. Body Back
3. Side of Head
4. Snout
5. Arm
6. Leg
7. Ear
8. Paw Pad

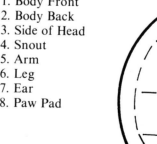

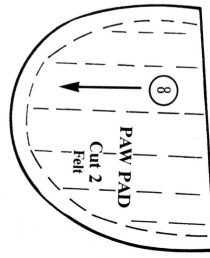

PAW PAD
Cut 2
Felt

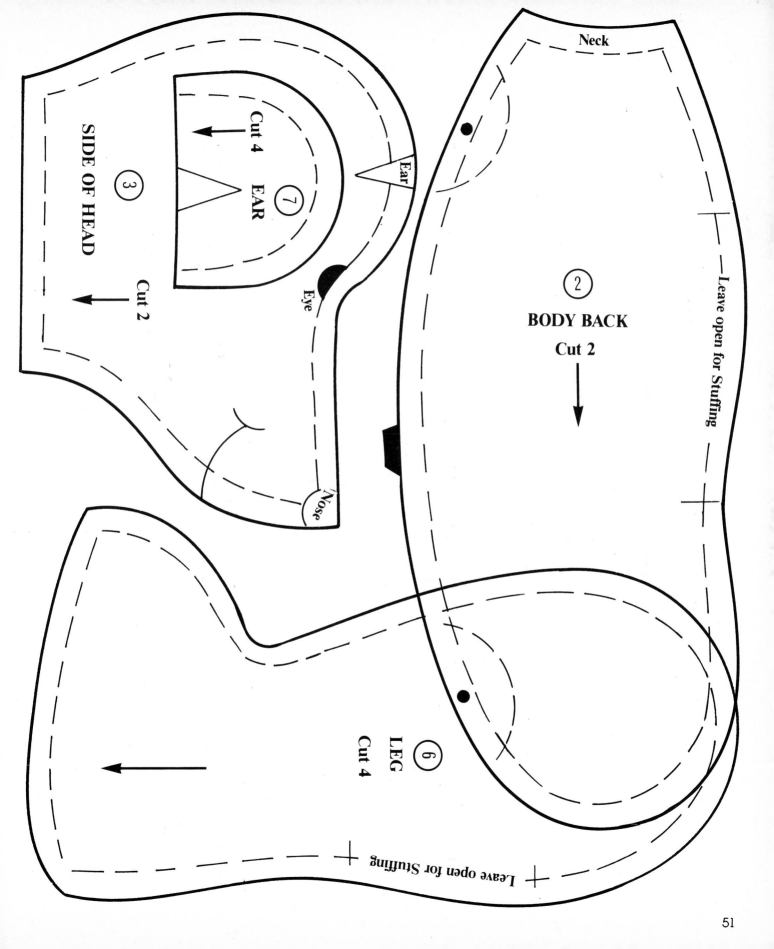

SIDE OF HEAD

③

Cut 2

Cut 4

⑦ EAR

Ear

Eye

Nose

Neck

②

BODY BACK

Cut 2

Leave open for Stuffing

⑥

LEG

Cut 4

Leave open for Stuffing

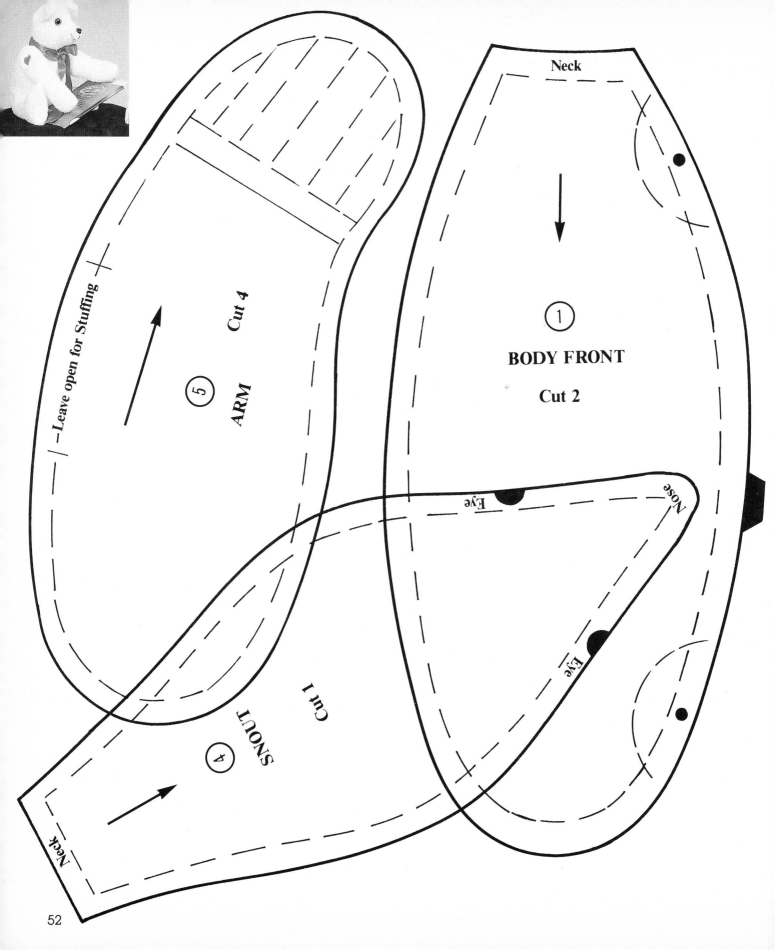

Neck

ARM

⑤

Cut 4

|– Leave open for Stuffing

BODY FRONT

①

Cut 2

Neck

Eye

Nose

Eye

SNOUT

④

Cut 1

Neck

52

Corduroy Bear

Corduroy Bear loves to tell jokes. He doesn't know that many, so you'll have to help him out with a few of your own. Elephant jokes are his favorite, but he enjoys listening to any joke you'll tell him. See page 84.

Treasure Bear

Treasure Bear is a pirate's partner. He will store all your most valuable finds and never tell anyone what or where they are. He loves treasure hunts, rock hunting, and playing hide and seek. See page 80.

Best Friend

Best Friend Bear is a good listener. He is quiet and can be taken anywhere you go. He never makes a fuss and loves to be hugged. See page 57.

BEST FRIEND BEAR

Size
App. 19¾" tall.

Materials
½ yard fleece, 54" wide; light brown felt; purchased eyes, (½"); purchased nose; 8 hardboard discs; 4 cotter pins for arm and leg joints; a "growler" mechanism (optional), brown thread; one large bag of polyester stuffing. Tracing or tissue paper.

Directions
Trace the pattern pieces on tracing paper as shown on suggested layout diagram, then pin the tracing paper to the wrong side of fabric. Make sure all pieces follow the arrows drawn on them, with the nap in a downward position. From fleece cut one each: back body, center of head, and snout. Cut 2 each: sides of head (1 reversed), body front (1 reversed). Cut 4 ears, 4 arms (2 reversed), 4 legs (2 reversed). From felt, cut 2 inner ears and 2 paw pads without seam allowance. Cut 2 foot pieces with seam allowance. Sew all pieces with right sides together.

Arms and Legs
Mark position for joints on the under arm and leg pieces. Punch hole for cotter pins with an awl or ice pick. Sew arm seams, leaving opening for turning and stuffing. Sew felt sole to leg. Turn arms and legs and stuff half full.

Head
Sew felt inner ear pieces to right side of 2 ear pieces. With right sides together sew outer ears together, leaving lower edge open for turning and stuffing. Turn right side out. Sew darts in the side of head pieces. With right sides together sew sides of head to center head piece, leaving neck edge open. Sew center seam and the round nose seam of muzzle. Place plastic nose in muzzle. Sew muzzle to head where indicated on center head piece, stuffing as you go. (See page 19.) Insert eyes at the side of head seams above muzzle.

Body
Mark position for joints. Punch hole for cotter pins with an awl or ice pick. Sew center seam of body front, leaving opening for turning and stuffing. Sew center seam of body back. Sew front to back at side seams. Turn body right side out. Cut a piece of cotton fabric to fit over the holes on the growler to keep the stuffing from blocking the holes. Stuff the body half full and set growler at the center of body. Sew head to body.

Joints
You'll need 4 sets of cotter pins and 4 hardboard discs. Insert cotter pin through one disc, through the arm, through the body, and through another disc. Bend ends of cotter pins tightly in place. Do the same with the other arm and the legs.

Finishing
Finish stuffing arms, legs and body. Close by hand. With brown thread, embroider the mouth with a stem stitch.

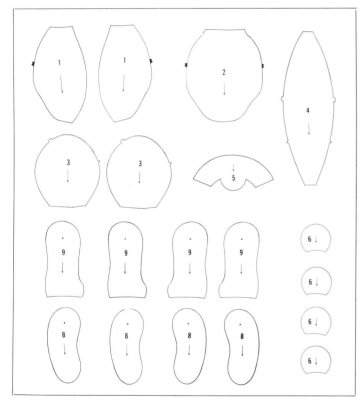

Felt

1. Body Front
2. Body Back
3. Side of Head
4. Center Head
5. Snout
6. Ear
7. Inner Ear
8. Arm
9. Leg
10. Paw Pad
11. Foot

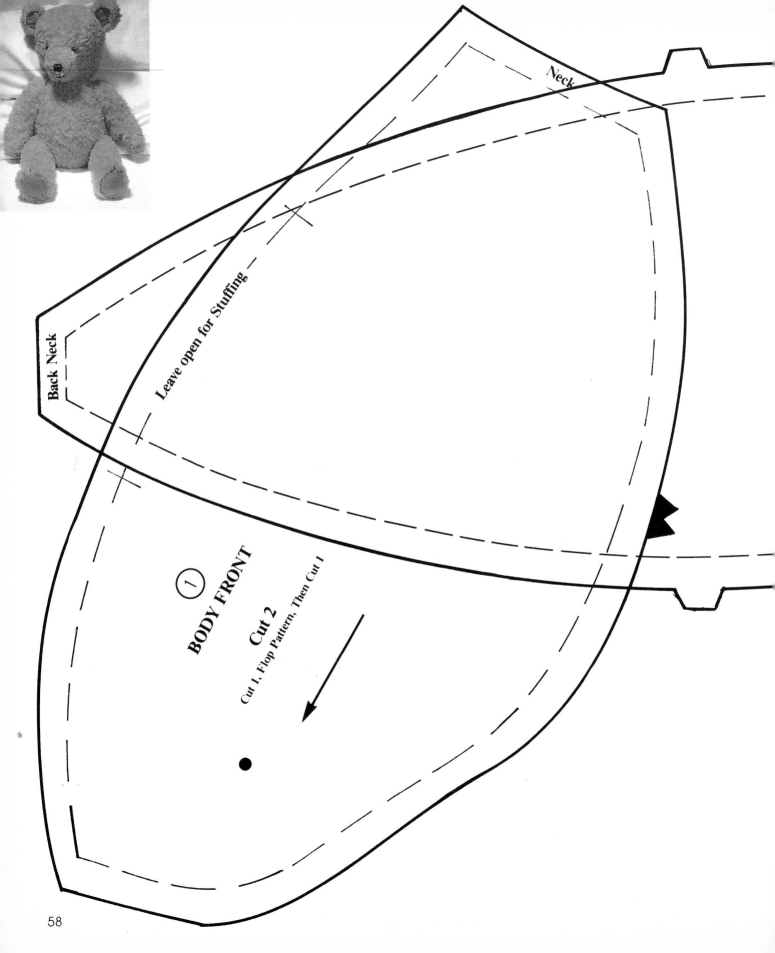

Neck

Back Neck

Leave open for Stuffing

BODY FRONT

①

Cut 2

Cut 1, Flop Pattern, Then Cut 1

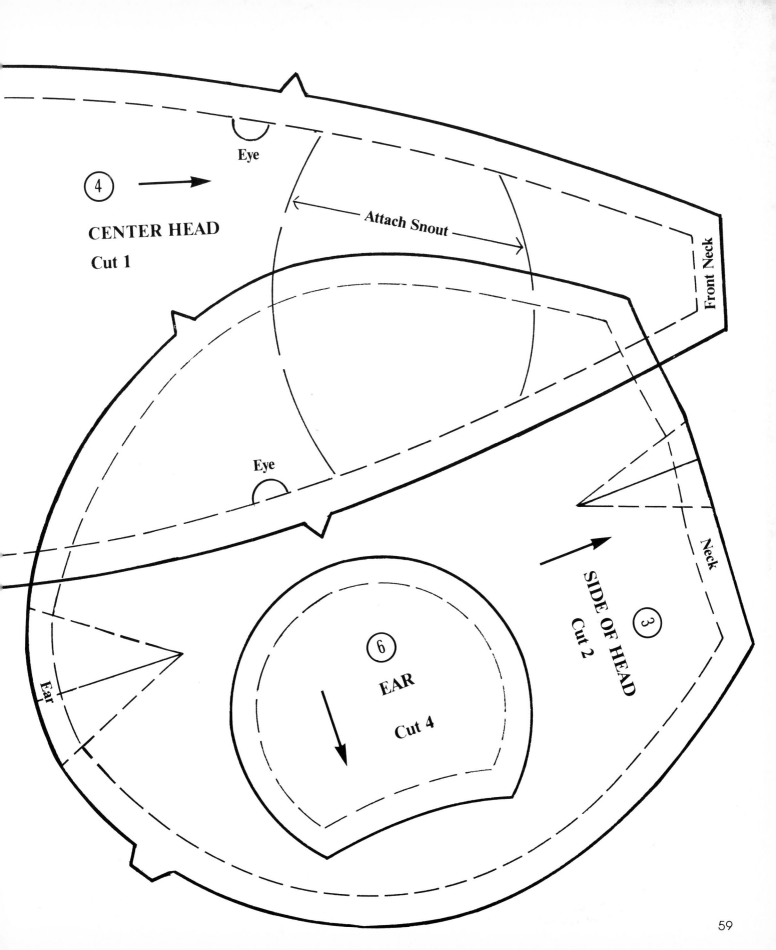

Eye

④ ➔

CENTER HEAD

Cut 1

Attach Snout

Front Neck

Eye

Neck

③

SIDE OF HEAD

Cut 2

➔

Ear

⑥

EAR

Cut 4

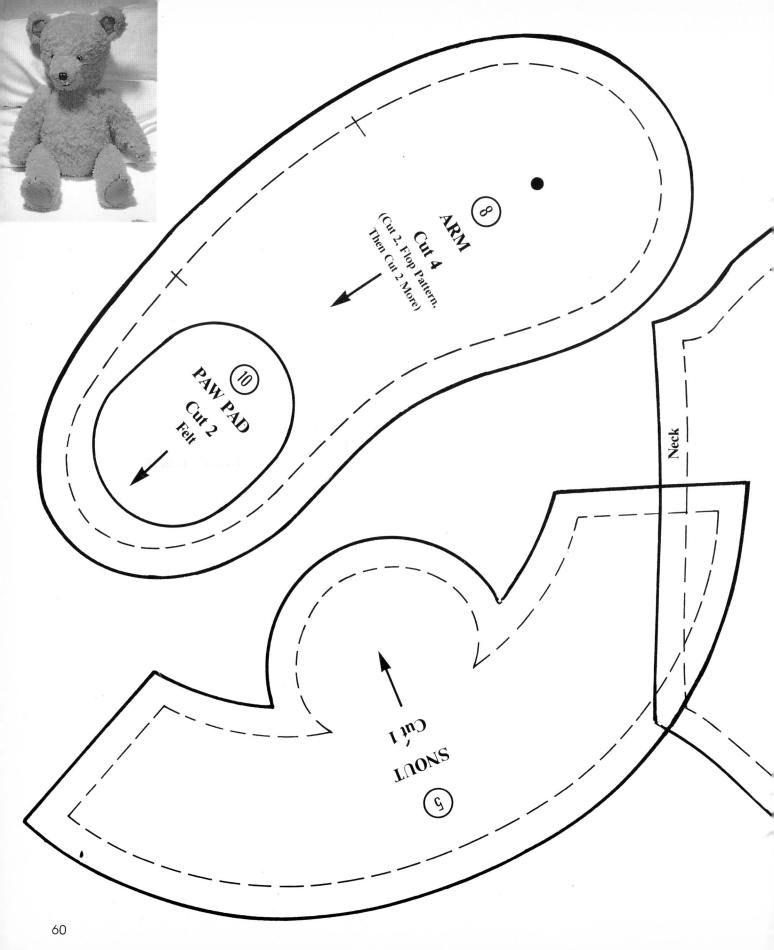

ARM
Cut 4
(Cut 2, Flop Pattern,
Then Cut 2 More)
⑧

PAW PAD
Cut 2
Felt
⑩

Neck

SNOUT
Cut 1
⑤

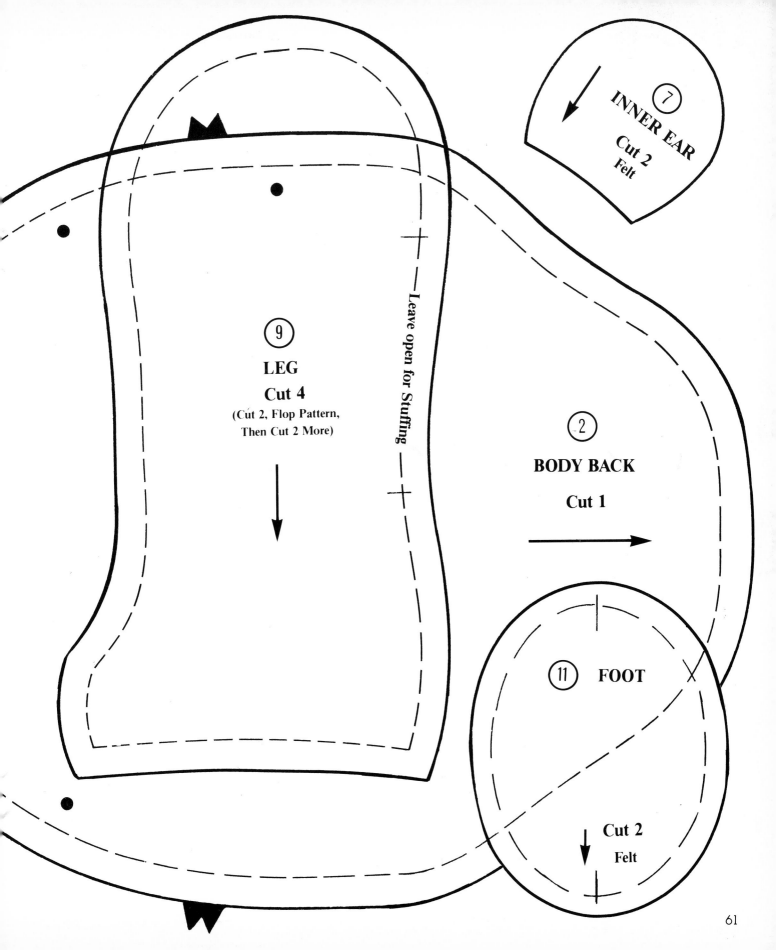

⑦ INNER EAR
Cut 2
Felt

⑨
LEG
Cut 4
(Cut 2, Flop Pattern,
Then Cut 2 More)

Leave open for Stuffing

② BODY BACK
Cut 1

⑪ FOOT
Cut 2
Felt

61

PANDA BEAR

Size
App. 15" tall.

Materials
20" x 18" white fleece; 22" x 16" black fleece; purchased safety eyes; pur-chased plastic safety nose, heavy duty thread; 8 large buttons with 2 holes; large sewing needle; large bag of poly-ester stuffing; tissue or tracing paper.

Directions

Trace pattern pieces on tracing paper. Then pin the tracing paper to the wrong side of fabric as shown on suggested lay-out diagram, making sure all pieces follow the arrows drawn on them, with the nap in a down-ward position. On white fleece, cut 2 pieces each: side of head (1 reversed), back of head (1 reversed), and soles. Cut 4 pieces of body front and back (2 reversed). Cut 1 piece for snout on folded white fleece. On black fleece cut 2 eye pieces (1 reversed). Cut 4 pieces each: arms (2 reversed), legs (2 reversed), and ears. Sew all pieces with right sides together.

Head
With right sides together sew the ears leaving lower edge open. Turn right side out and stuff. Sew the darts on the side of head pieces. Baste ears in place. Sew black eye pieces to side of head matching notches. Set plastic eyes in black eye pieces where indicated. Sew center seam of side of head. With fold of snout at center seam sew snout to head. Sew center seam of snout. Attach nose. Sew the back of head darts and sew center seam. Sew the back and side of head pieces together.

Arms and Legs
Mark joint placement in under arm and under leg where indicated. With right sides together sew arm seams, leaving opening for turning and stuffing. Sew leg seams, except bottom seam, leaving opening in side seam for turning and stuffing. Sew in soles. Turn arms and legs right side out and stuff half full.

Body
Sew the center seam of the front and back body pieces, leaving an opening for turning and stuffing in the front center seam. Sew the side and lower seam leaving the neck edge open. Sew the head to the body and turn right side out. Stuff the head and then the body half full.

Finishing
Thread a piece of white sewing thread through 1 hole of a button, then the other hole of button and slide the button to the middle of the thread. Thread both ends of the thread through the needle. Place the button on inside of one arm and sew back and forth through the fabric of the arm and the body at indicated places, then sew through holes of a second button placed inside body. Continue to

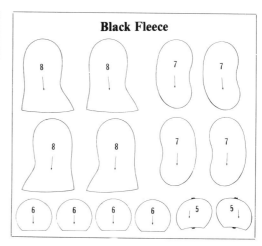

White Fleece

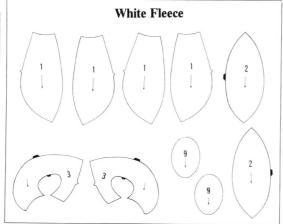

Black Fleece

White Fleece
1. Body Front and Back
2. Back of Head
3. Side of Head
4. Snout
9. Foot

Black Fleece
5. Eye
6. Ear
7. Arm
8. Leg

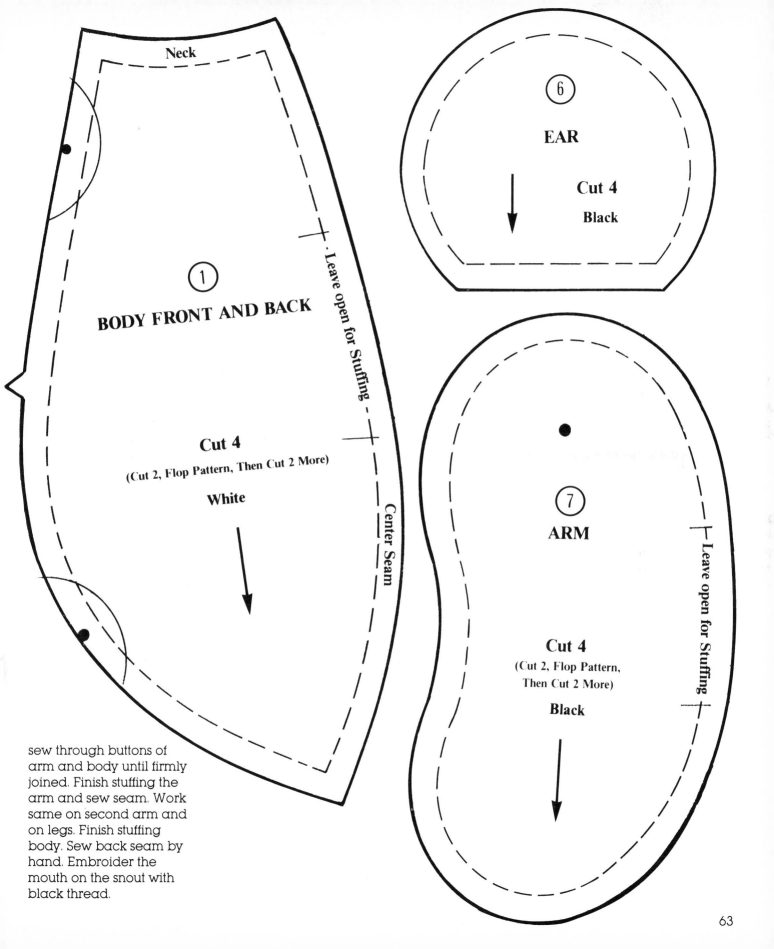

Neck

① BODY FRONT AND BACK

Cut 4
(Cut 2, Flop Pattern, Then Cut 2 More)

White

Leave open for Stuffing

Center Seam

⑥ EAR

Cut 4

Black

⑦ ARM

Cut 4
(Cut 2, Flop Pattern,
Then Cut 2 More)

Black

Leave open for Stuffing

sew through buttons of arm and body until firmly joined. Finish stuffing the arm and sew seam. Work same on second arm and on legs. Finish stuffing body. Sew back seam by hand. Embroider the mouth on the snout with black thread.

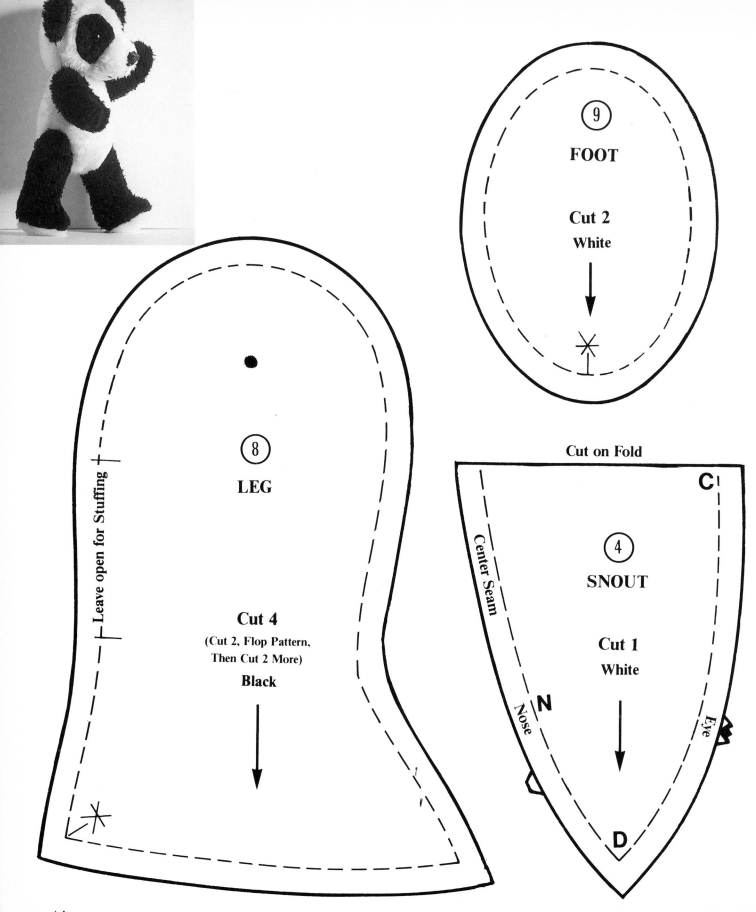

⑨

FOOT

Cut 2
White

Leave open for Stuffing

⑧

LEG

Cut 4
(Cut 2, Flop Pattern,
Then Cut 2 More)

Black

Cut on Fold

C

Center Seam

④

SNOUT

Cut 1
White

Nose

N

Eye

D

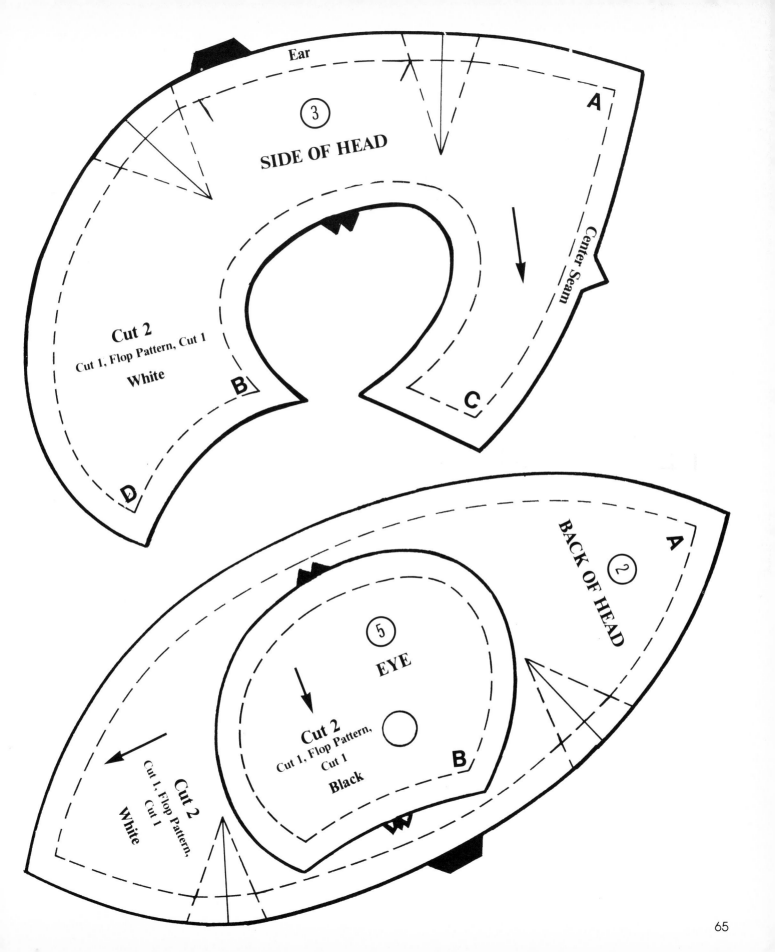

Ear

③

SIDE OF HEAD

Cut 2
Cut 1, Flop Pattern, Cut 1

White

A

Center Seam

B

C

D

A

BACK OF HEAD

②

⑤

EYE

Cut 2
Cut 1, Flop Pattern,
Cut 1

Black

B

Cut 2
Cut 1, Flop Pattern,
Cut 1

White

BROWN BEAR

Size
App. 25½" tall.

Materials
1 yard dark brown fabric, 45" wide; small piece medium brown felt; large purchased button eyes; purchased plastic nose; one large bag of polyester stuffing; 8 hardboard discs; 4 cotter pins; brown or black embroidery floss, tissue or tracing paper.

Directions

Trace the pattern pieces on tissue paper. Then pin the tissue paper to the wrong side of fabric as shown on suggested layout diagram. Make sure all pieces follow the arrows drawn on them, with the nap in a downward position. On doubled brown fabric cut 4 ears, 4 arms (2 reversed), 4 legs (2 reversed). Cut 2 pieces of the bear body back, body front, back of head, and side head pieces. Cut 2 soles. On felt cut 1 muzzle, 2 inner ears, 2 paw pads and 2 foot pads.

Arms and Legs
Punch hole in under arm and leg for cotter pins with an ice pick or awl. Sew felt paw pads on under arm pieces where indicated. With right sides together sew seams leaving an opening for stuffing and turning. Sew darts in the bottom of legs. With right sides together sew seams leaving an opening for stuffing and turning. Sew felt pad to bottom of foot. Sew foot in leg. Turn arms and legs right side out and stuff half full.

Ears
Sew felt inner ear pieces to right side of 2 outer ears. With right sides together sew outer ear seams leaving lower edge open. Turn right side out and stuff.

Head
Sew all darts in side of head. Sew muzzle to sides of head. Fold at muzzle and close chin. Put in eyes and nose. Sew center seam of back of head pieces. Baste ears in place where indicated on side of head pieces. Sew back of head to side of head pieces.

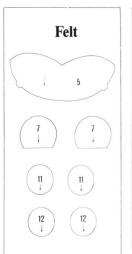

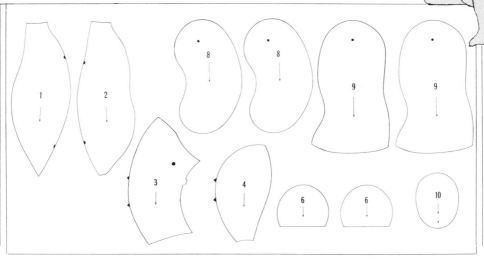

Felt

1. Body Front
2. Body Back
3. Side of Head
4. Back of Head
5. Muzzle
6. Ear
7. Inner Ear
8. Arm
9. Leg
10. Foot
11. Foot Pad
12. Paw Pad

Body

With right sides together, sew the bear back at center seam. Sew front sides to side seams of back. Sew center seam of body front, leaving opening for turning and stuffing. Sew body front to body back at side seams. Turn body right side out. Sew head to body by matching neck and body seams.

Joints

You'll need 4 sets of cotter pins and 4 hardboard discs. Insert cotter pin through one disc, through the arm, through the body and through another disc. Bend ends of cotter pins tightly in place. Do the same with the other arm and the legs. Finish stuffing legs, arms and body. Close by hand.

Finishing

Add the mouth by following the muzzle seams with black embroidery thread.

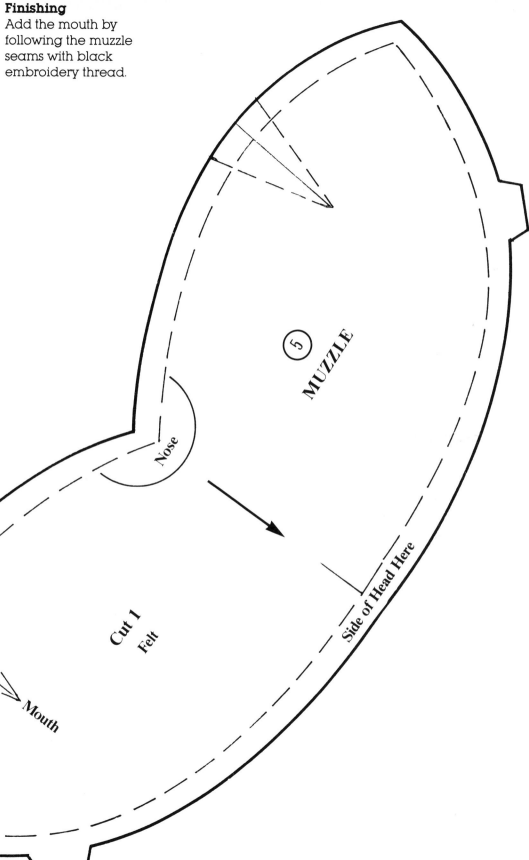

MUZZLE
⑤
Nose
Cut 1
Felt
Mouth
Side of Head Here

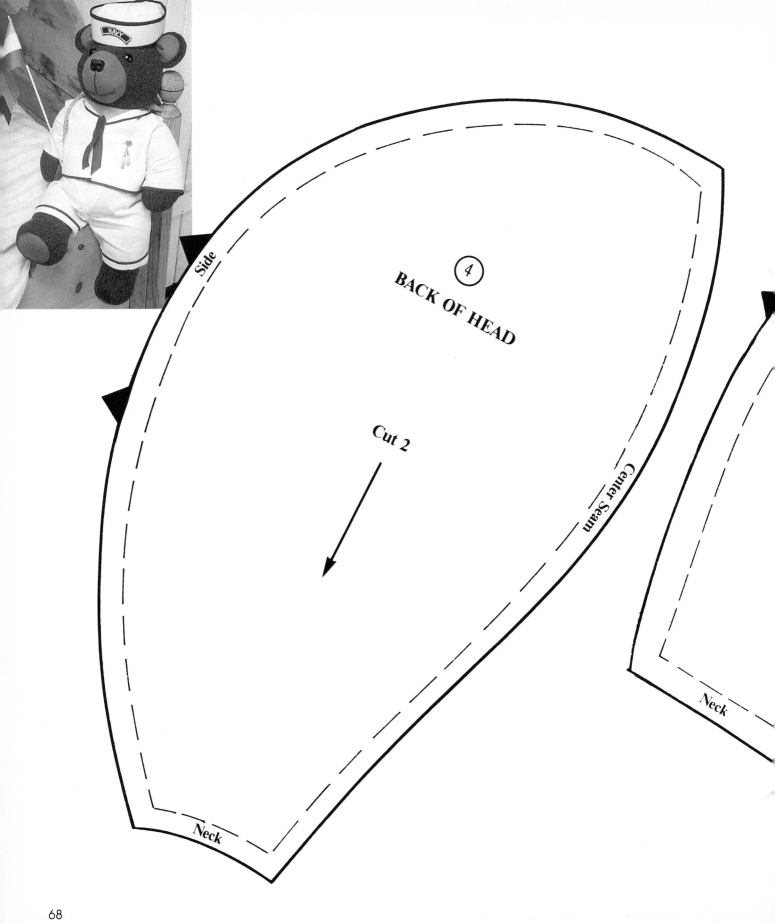

Side

④
BACK OF HEAD

Cut 2

Center Seam

Neck

Neck

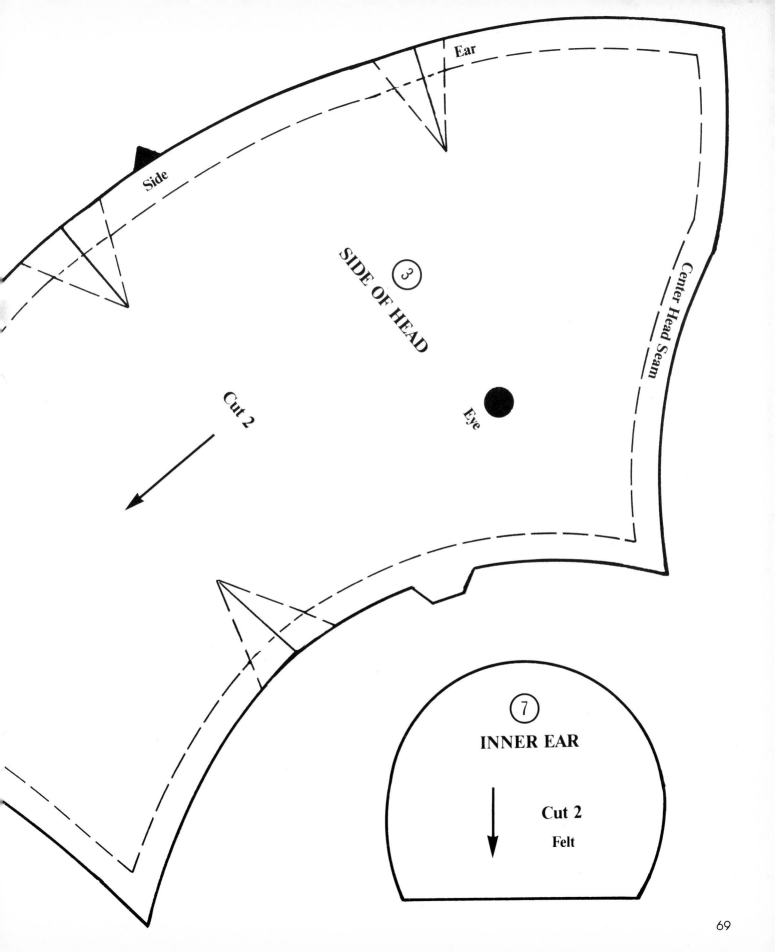

Ear

Side

③

SIDE OF HEAD

Cut 2

Eye

Center Head Seam

⑦

INNER EAR

Cut 2

Felt

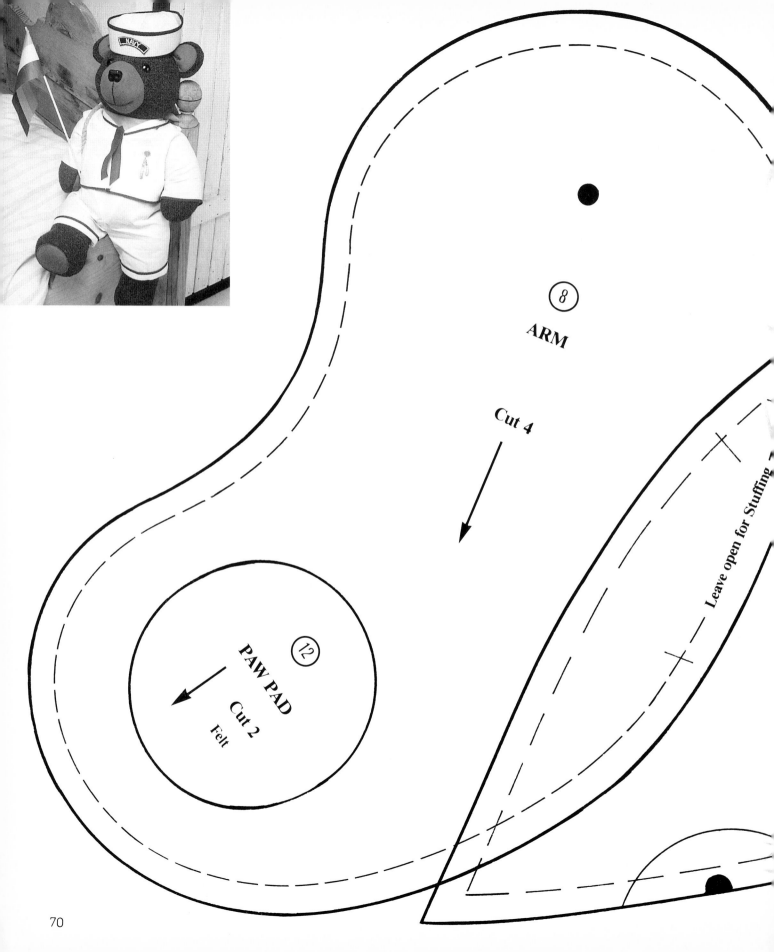

⑧

ARM

Cut 4

Leave open for Stuffing

⑫

PAW PAD

Cut 2

Felt

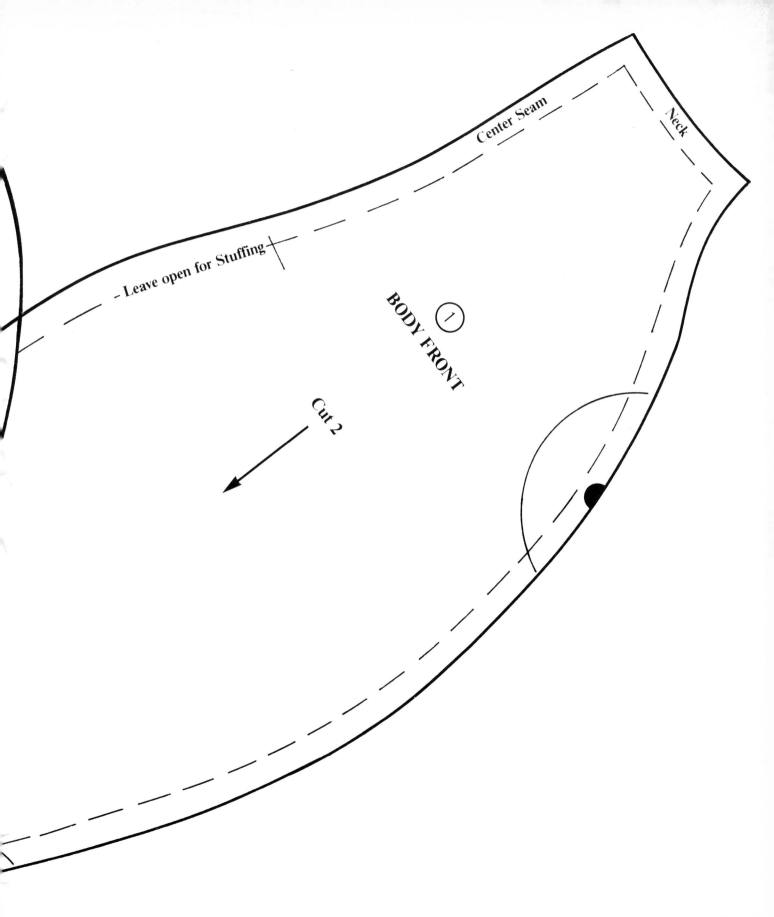

Center Seam

Neck

Leave open for Stuffing

BODY FRONT

①

Cut 2

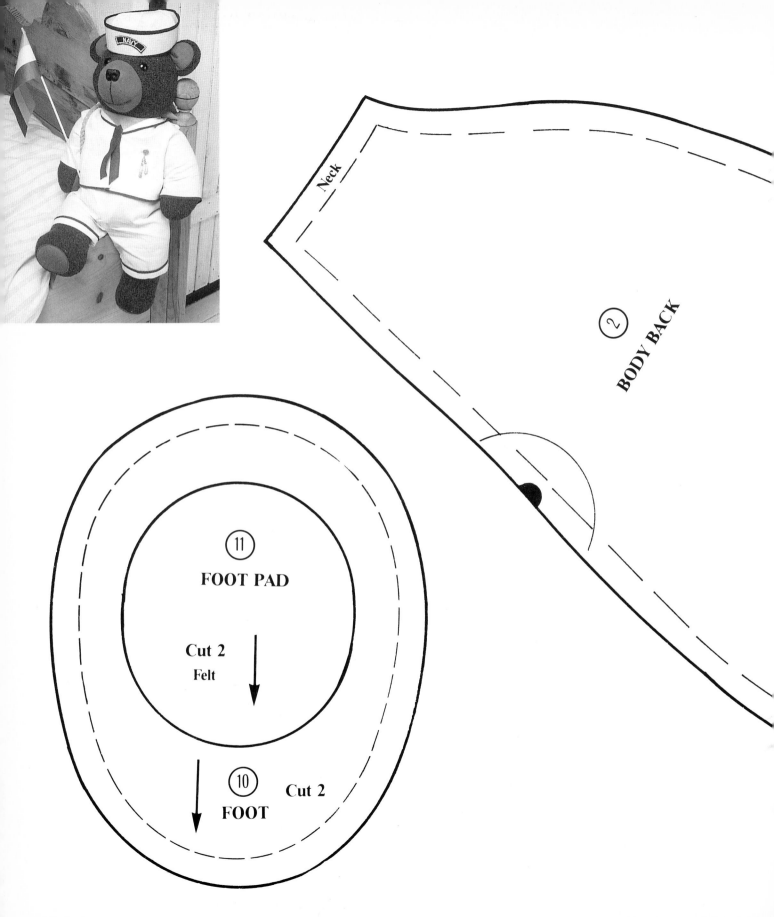

Neck

② BODY BACK

⑪ FOOT PAD

Cut 2

Felt

⑩ FOOT

Cut 2

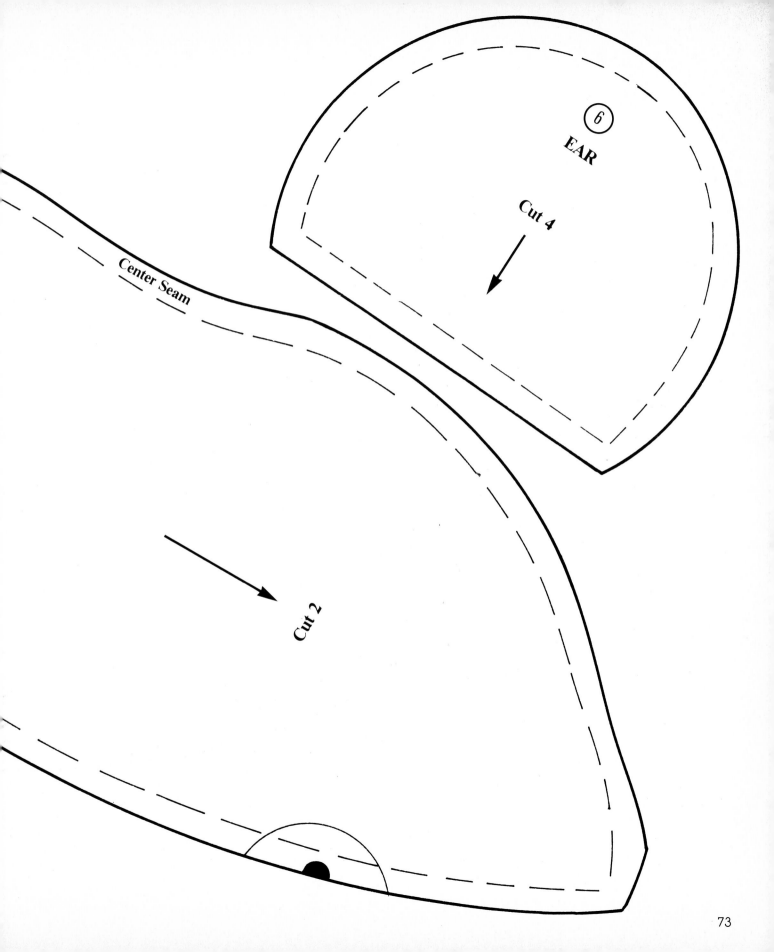

⑥

EAR

Cut 4

Center Seam

Cut 2

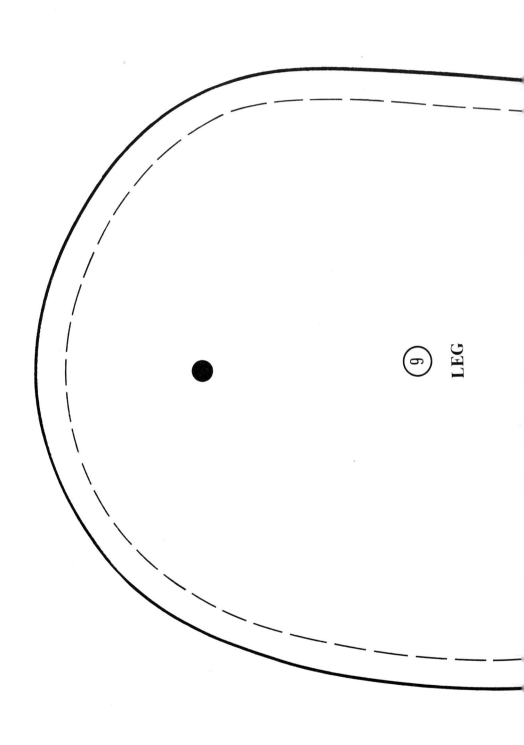

⑨ LEG

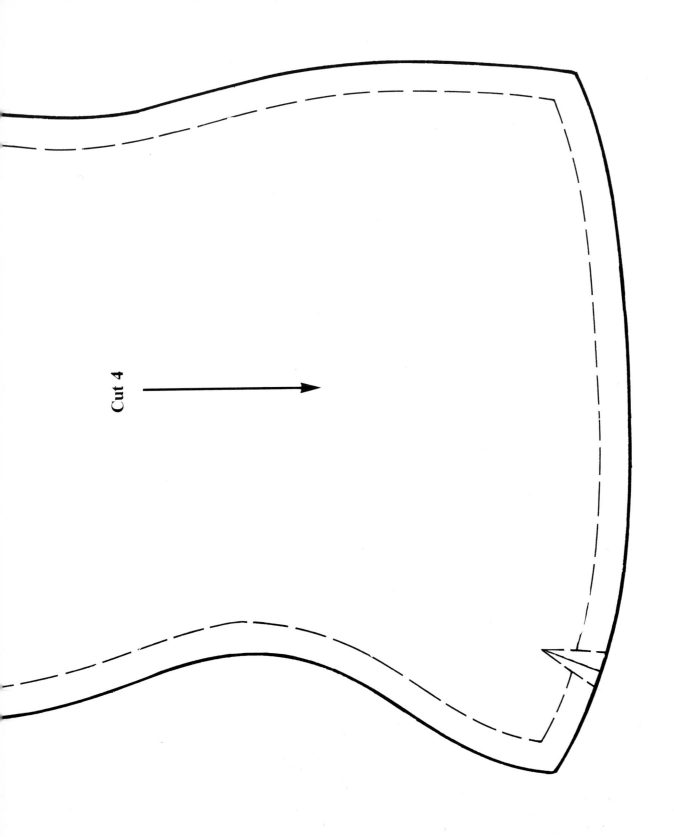

Cut 4

PETIE POLAR BEAR

Size
App. 14½" tall.

Materials
1/3 yard white short nap fur fabric, 54" wide; 6" x 8" piece of gray felt; small amount of black felt; gray and white embroidery thread; 8 large buttons with 2 holes; heavy duty thread; large bag of polyester stuffing, tissue or tracing paper.

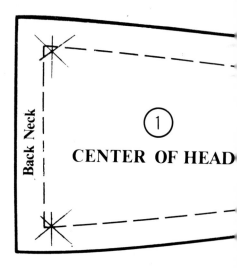

Directions

Trace the pattern pieces on tracing paper. Then pin the tracing paper to the wrong side of the fabric as shown on suggested layout digram. Make sure all pieces follow the arrows drawn on them, with the nap in a downward position.

On the fur fabric cut 2 each of the sides of the head, the middle of the body, the sides of the body, the ears and the soles of the feet. Cut 1 each of the center of the head and snout. Cut 4 arms (2 reversed) and 4 legs (2 reversed). On the gray felt cut 2 ears, 2 foot pads, and 2 paw pads. Sew all pieces with right sides together.

Head
Mark and sew the darts on the side of the head pieces. With right sides together, sew the center piece to the side pieces. Turn the head right side out. With right sides together, sew the lower edges of snout, from point A to point B. Let this seam be the center of the snout as indicated on pattern piece. Turn snout right side out. Stuff the snout and sew to head as indicated on the pattern pieces. Embroider the nose using 3 strands of gray embroidery floss in satin stitch, embroider the mouth in stem stitch and the whisker dots in satin stitch. With right sides together, sew pieces of ears (1 of felt, 1 of fabric) together, leaving the lower edge open. Turn right side out. Turn lower edge to inside and baste. Sew ears to head as indicated on pattern pieces. For the eyes, cut 2 circles about 1/4" in diameter of gray felt, then for the pupils, cut 2 circles about 1/5" in diameter of black felt. Sew the pupils to the eyes and sew to the head. With white embroidery floss, embroider the pupils in satin stitch as shown in photo.

Body
Sew the side pieces to center back and front, right sides together, leaving the center back edge open for about 3" to turn. Mark the 4 points where the legs and arms fit. Sew head to neck of bear, turn right side out and stuff.

Arms and Legs
With right sides together, sew the arms, leaving the straight sides open. Turn to right side, stuff half full. Sew leg seams except bottom, leaving side open for turning. Sew in soles. Turn to right side and stuff half full.

Finishing
Thread a piece of white heavy duty thread through 1 hole of a button, then the other hole of button and slide the button to the middle of the thread. Thread both ends of the heavy duty thread through the needle. Place the button on inside of one arm and

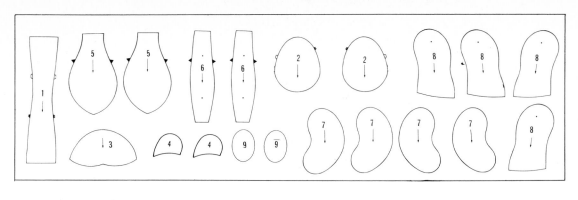

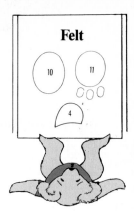

Felt

1. Center of Head
2. Side of Head
3. Snout

4. Ear
5. Body Middle
6. Body Side

7. Arm
8. Leg
9. Foot

10. Paw Pad
11. Foot Pad

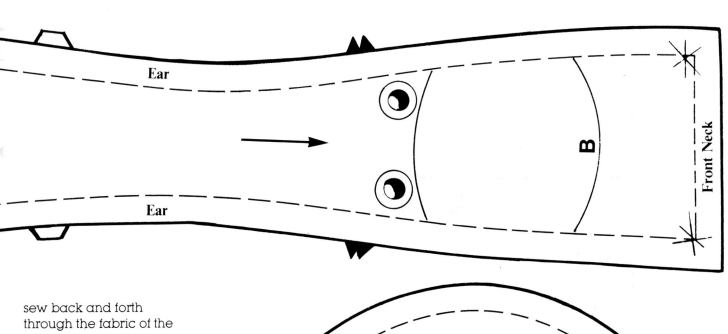

Ear

Ear

Front Neck

B

sew back and forth through the fabric of the arm and the body at indicated places, then sew through holes of a second button placed inside body. Continue to sew through buttons of arm and body until firmly joined. Work same on second arm and on legs. Finish stuffing arms and legs and close by hand. Finish stuffing body. Sew back seam. Sew felt to palms and soles of feet. Embroider claws on paws in satin stitch.

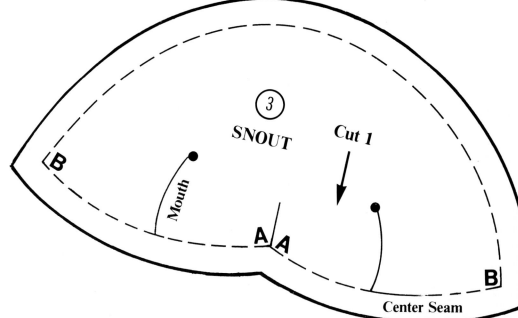

③ SNOUT   Cut 1

B

Mouth

A A

B

Center Seam

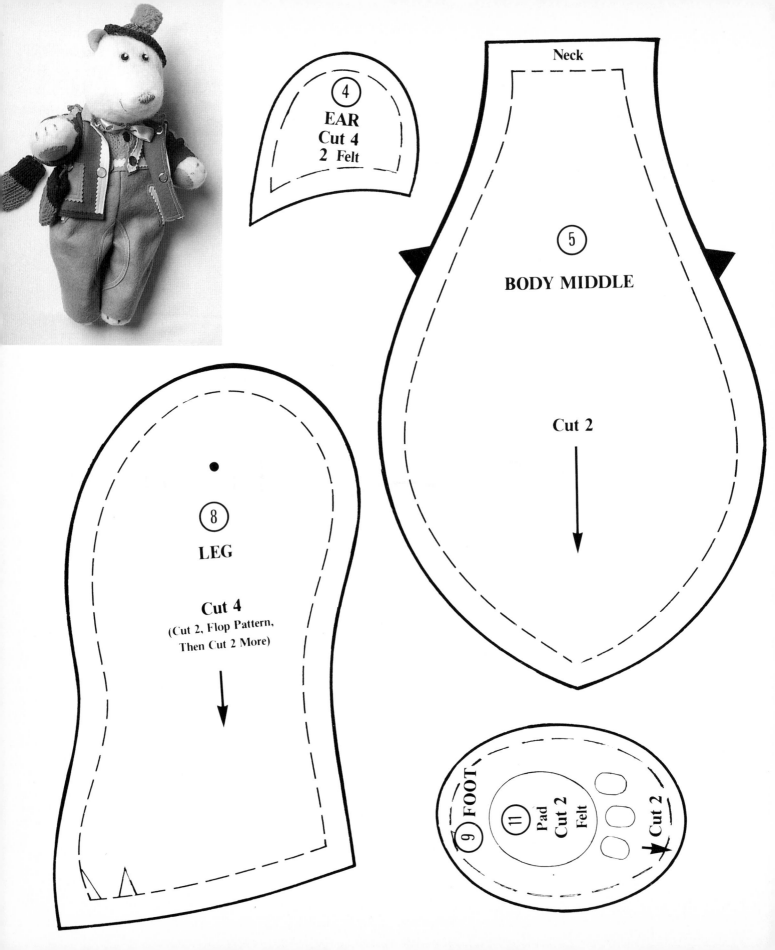

④
EAR
Cut 4
2 Felt

Neck

⑤
BODY MIDDLE

Cut 2

⑧
LEG

Cut 4
(Cut 2, Flop Pattern,
Then Cut 2 More)

⑨ FOOT

⑪
Pad
Cut 2
Felt

Cut 2

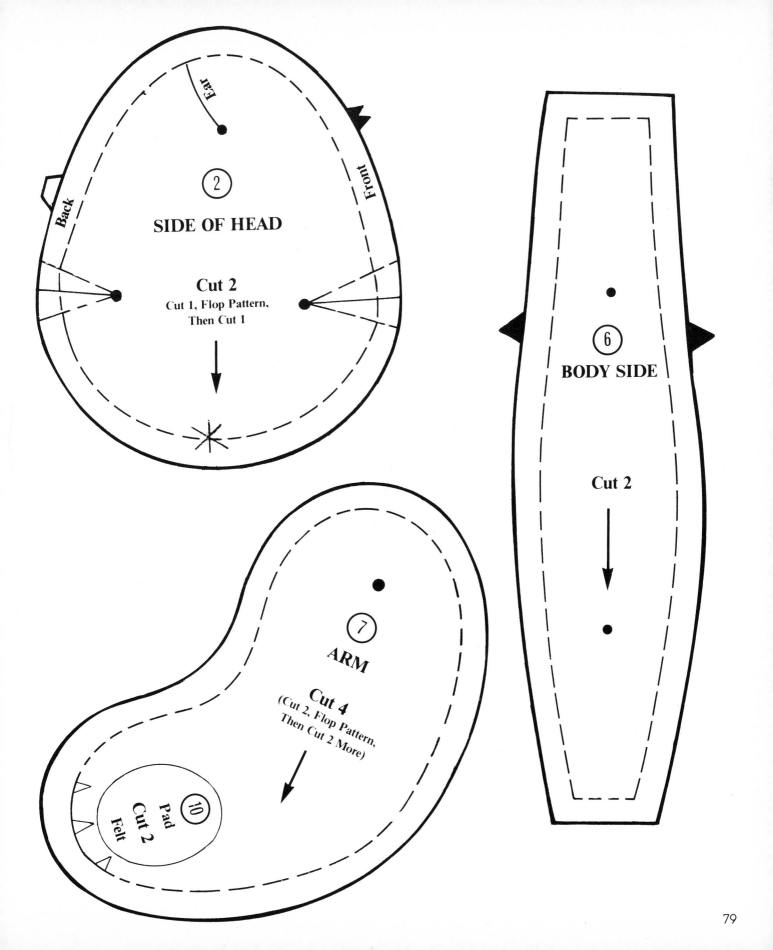

Ear

Back

Front

②

SIDE OF HEAD

Cut 2
Cut 1, Flop Pattern,
Then Cut 1

⑥

BODY SIDE

Cut 2

⑦

ARM

Cut 4
(Cut 2, Flop Pattern,
Then Cut 2 More)

⑩
Pad
Cut 2
Felt

TREASURE BEAR

Size
App. 13" tall.

Materials
½ yard short fur. Purchased eyes and nose. Two pieces of 4" x 6" red satin. ¾ yard of red ribbon. One 6" zipper to match fur color. One ¾" red heart shaped button. Red embroidery thread.

Directions

Trace pattern pieces on tissue paper. Cut out pattern and lay it on the wrong side of the fur as shown on suggested layout diagram. Make sure the arrows are with the nap in a downward position. Cut 1 front right, then flip over and cut 1 front left. Cut 1 backside, then flip over and cut other side, making the back 1 piece.

Cut 1 side, flop pattern and cut the other side, making the back one piece.

Eyes

Punch holes with awl and insert eyes.

Body

Start at the top of the head and sew seams together to end of snout. Then drop down ¼″ for nose and continue sewing to belly notch. Leave opening for zipper. Finish sewing to crotch. Sew zipper. Sew satin on each side of zipper to make pocket. Close both ends leaving one side of satin open and pull back through belly to keep out of the way. Sew front and back together. Turn bear through belly.

Ears

Sew across the top of the head to separate the ears. Stuff head, neck, arms, and legs lightly.

Topstitch

Topstitch the arms and legs as marked on pattern and finish stuffing bear body. Close your pocket with fusible tape or stitch closed.

Mouth

Embroider mouth about ¾″ from under the nose in seam.

Button

Sew button to zipper tab. Add red ribbon. Your Treasure Bear is finished. Treasure Bear is a nice gift and when you add a surprise, it makes it all worthwhile.

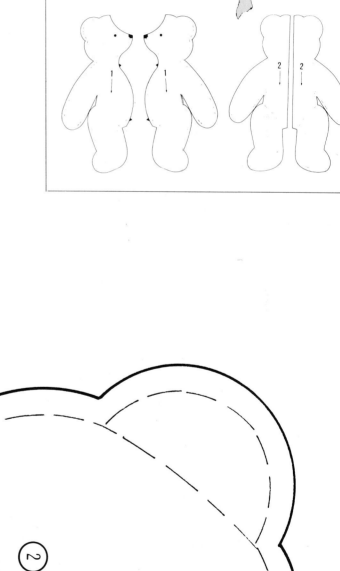

BACK ②

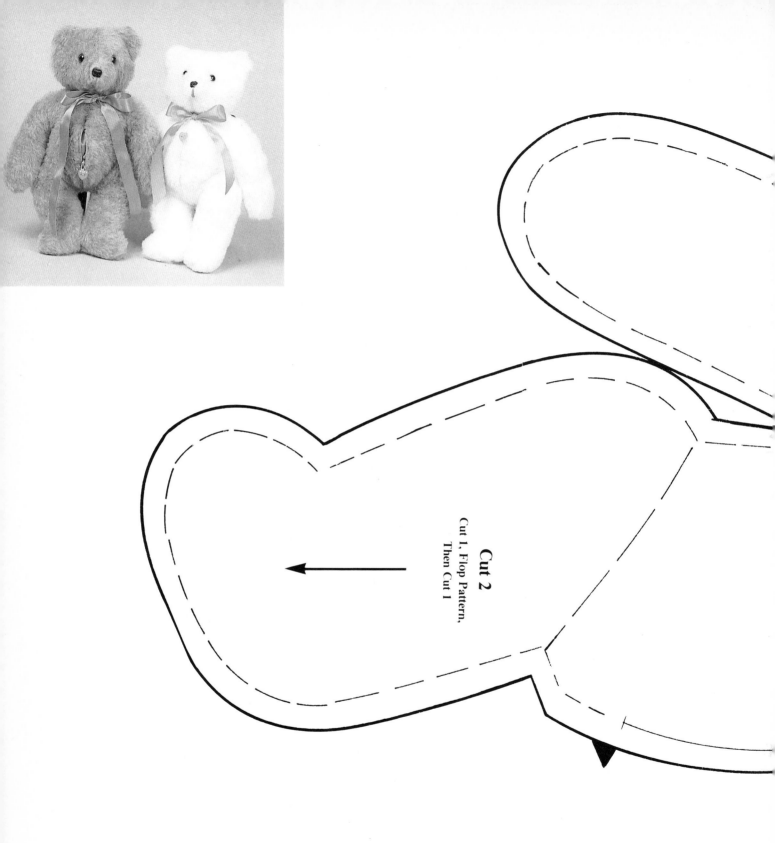

Cut 2
Cut 1, Flop Pattern,
Then Cut 1

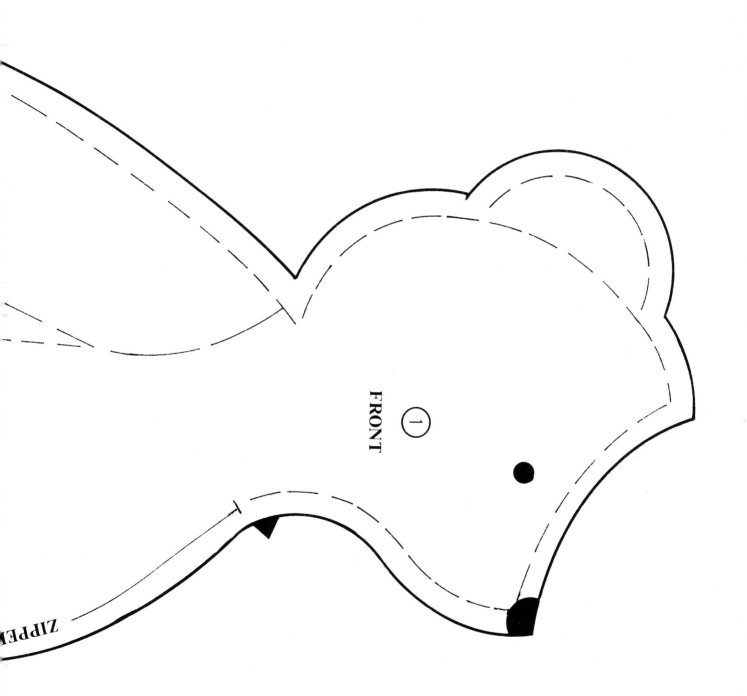

FRONT

①

ZIPPE

CORDUROY BEAR

Size
App. 15¾" tall.

Materials
½ yard brown corduroy, 45" wide; large bag of polyester stuffing; 2 purchased eyes; purchased nose; black embroidery thread; 8 hardboard discs; 4 cotter pins; tracing or tissue paper.

Directions

Trace the pattern pieces on tracing paper. Then pin the tracing paper to the wrong side of fabric, as shown on suggested layout diagram. Make sure all pieces follow the arrows drawn on them, with the nap in a downward position. On doubled fabric cut 2 pieces of the bear body back, body front, back of head, and side head pieces. Cut 2 soles of the foot out of the same fabric or a contrasting fabric such as felt, leather, or the reverse of the fabric being used for the bear. Cut 4 ears, 4 arms (2 reversed), 4 legs (2 reversed). Cut 1 upper and 1 lower snout.

Arms and Legs
Punch a hole in the arms, legs, and body for cotter pins with an ice pick or an awl. With right sides together sew arms, leaving an opening for stuffing and turning. Sew leg seams leaving an opening in side for turning. Sew pad to bottom of foot. Sew bottom of foot in leg. Turn arms and legs right side out and stuff.

Ears
With right sides together, sew ears leaving the bottom open for stuffing and turning. Ears can be topstitched ¼" if desired.

Head
Sew upper and lower snout to the side of the bear's head. Pin ears in place. Set your eyes and nose at this time. Sew back of head to side of head, turn.

Body
With right sides together, sew the bear back center seam, leaving an opening for turning. Sew front sides to side seams of back. Sew front center seam. Sew head to body by matching your neck and body seams together. Insert your joints in bear body by punching the cotter pin through the body so it will be easily pushed into the arms and legs. Add arms and legs by connecting the joint to the body. When all joints are in place, it is time to stuff the bear and close the opening by making an invisible stitch.

Finishing
Your bear is ready for a mouth, which is easy, because this bear's mouth follow the seams. If you'd like, a ribbon can be added around his neck.

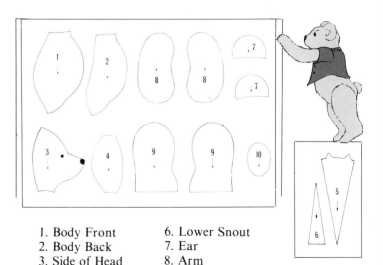

1. Body Front
2. Body Back
3. Side of Head
4. Back of Head
5. Upper Snout
6. Lower Snout
7. Ear
8. Arm
9. Leg
10. Foot

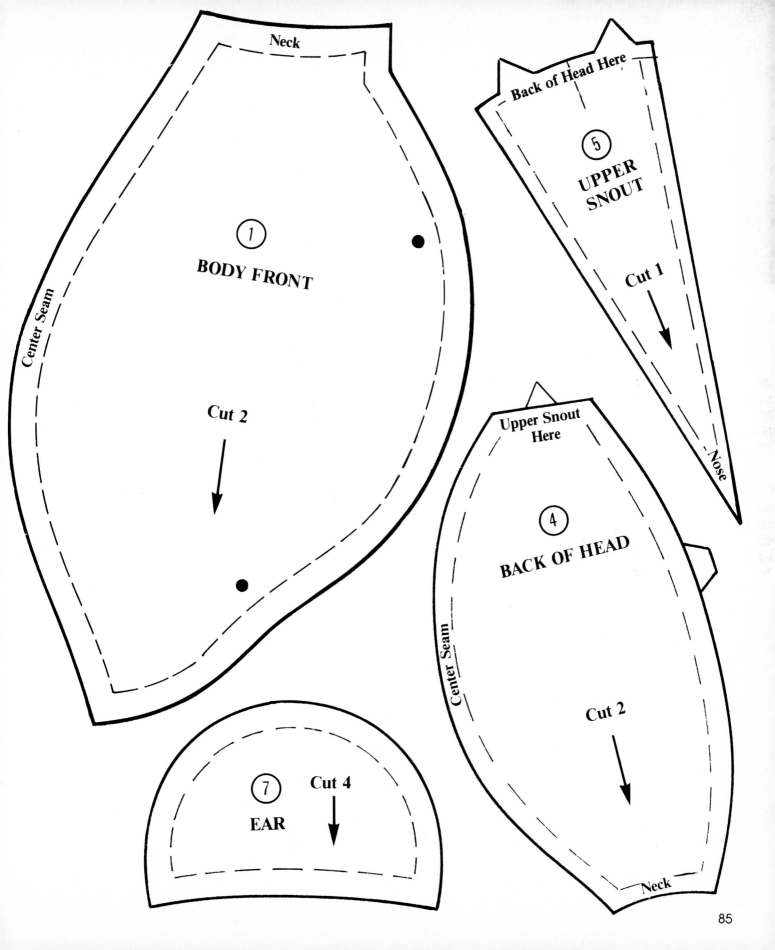

Neck

①
BODY FRONT

Center Seam

Cut 2

⑤
UPPER SNOUT

Back of Head Here

Cut 1

Nose

④
BACK OF HEAD

Upper Snout Here

Center Seam

Cut 2

Neck

⑦
EAR

Cut 4

85

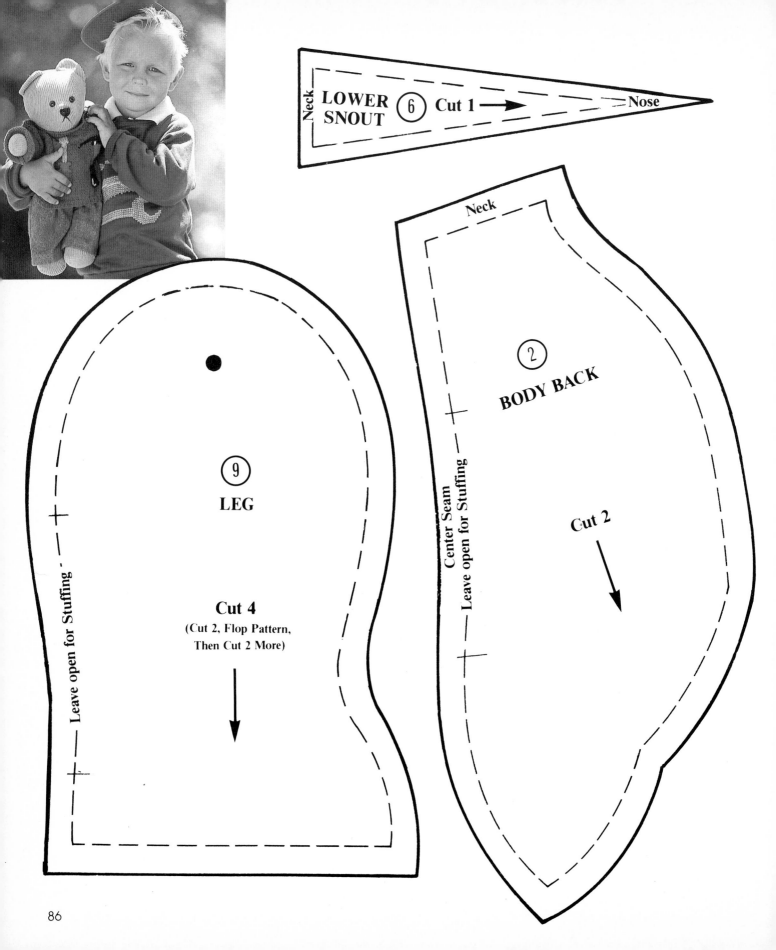

LOWER SNOUT ⑥ Cut 1 →

Neck

Nose

Neck

② BODY BACK

Center Seam
Leave open for Stuffing

Cut 2

⑨ LEG

Cut 4
(Cut 2, Flop Pattern,
Then Cut 2 More)

Leave open for Stuffing

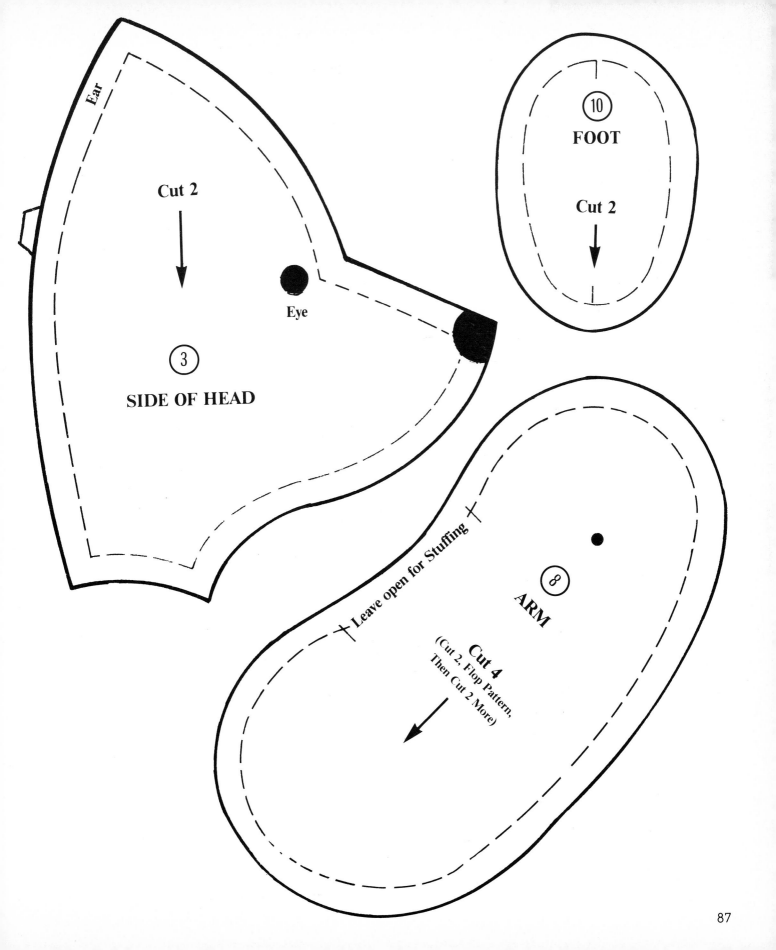

Ear

Cut 2 ↓

Eye

③

SIDE OF HEAD

⑩

FOOT

Cut 2 ↓

Leave open for Stuffing

⑧

ARM

Cut 4
(Cut 2, Flop Pattern,
Then Cut 2 More)

Scarf/Mitten Set

The bear scarf and mitten set not only surround a child with bears, it keeps them warm at the same time. See page 97.

89

Bear Purse

A little girl would love this bear purse. It's big enough to fit all of her necessities and a smiling, furry bear too! What more could she want? See page 98.

Bear Cushion

The dancing bears make a nice place for a child to relax while reading, coloring, or painting. See page 100.

Bear Hanger

This bear hanger is the only place to hang a child's winter coat while warming up inside the house after a hard day sledding, skiing, or snowball making. See page 101.

Cross-Stitched Hat Rack

*The cross-stitched bears offer
a warm haven for a raincoat,
hat, umbrella or book bag to
hang on until they're needed
again. See page 102.*

Bear Backpack

A nice, useful item for boys and girls. Your child will find numerous uses for the backpack: from school to home, trips to hiking, even a picnic in the park. See page 103.

Bear Rug

What child wouldn't enjoy receiving this bear rug as a gift? He's warm, soft, portable, and totally irresistible. You don't have to have a fireplace to give the bear a home. He'll be just as happy lying around the house, on a wall, or on the bed. See page 108.

Boris Bear

Boris is a good project for a rainy day. It not only gives a child something to make, it also gives them someone to play with while inside.

Directions

1. Trace the body, arms, and legs of Boris on tissue paper. Cut the pattern pieces out of different colored construction paper.
2. Glue the pieces on cardboard and cut out the pieces.
3. Make round holes where indicated.
4. Insert brads in the holes through the body and the larger holes on the legs and arms. Fold the ends of the brads so that the arms and legs move freely.
5. Thread string through the small holes on the arms. Knot the ends.
6. Thread string through the small holes on the legs. Knot the ends.
7. Cut a string 10" long and knot between the arms and legs. (see photo)
8. Attach a button to the end and make a knot to secure button.
9. Make a hole in Boris's head and knot a string through hole to hang up

BEAR SCARF AND MITTENS

Size
Scarf: 5½" x 37½".

Materials
Red knit fabric 17¾" x 39¼". Red knit fabric 4" x 9¾" for mittens. 8" piece of 1½" knit ribbing. Yellow plush fabric 10" x 14". Brown felt. White and black embroidery floss. Small amount of black cotton.

Directions

Scarf

Trace the pattern pieces on tracing paper. From the plush fabric, cut 2 head pieces and 8 ears. From the doubled felt, cut 1 snout and 4 inner ears. From red fabric cut 2 pieces 6¼ x 38", cutting the ends to correspond to the outline of the head.

Bear Head

Sew the center seam of snout. Sew on snout by hand to the head. Cut out the nose from black cotton and sew on by hand. Embroider the mouth using 2 strands of black embroidery floss in stem stitch. Embroider the eyes in satin stitch using 6 strands of black embroidery floss. Embroider the highlights in eyes using 2 strands of white. Sew on inner ear to 4 pieces of outer ears. Place front and back outer ears right sides together and sew around side and upper edges. Turn right

side out and sew to top of head. Place 1 head at each end of 1 piece of knit fabric, right sides together. Sew heads to fabric around side and lower seams. Place 2nd piece of fabric on first, right sides together and sew side seams, leaving an opening. Turn right side out and sew top of head to fabric.

Mittens

Trace the pattern pieces on tissue paper. Cut the bear pieces the same as scarf. Cut the mitten pieces from smaller piece of red fabric. Cut 2 pieces from doubled fabric. Place 2 pieces right sides together and sew along sides and bottom. Cut the 8" piece of knit ribbing in half.

Sew the end pieces of each 4" section right sides together and turn right side out. Sew to the top part of mittens.

Bear Head

Cut 2 head pieces from red knitted material. Sew on the inner ears to the outside of plush head. With right sides together, sew the plush and knitted heads together, leaving an opening to turn. Clip seams around ears and turn right side out. Sew on snout. Embroider the mouth in stem stitch in black, embroider the nose and eyes in satin stitch in black. Embroider eye highlights in white in satin stitch. Sew on heads to mittens, leaving the ears free.

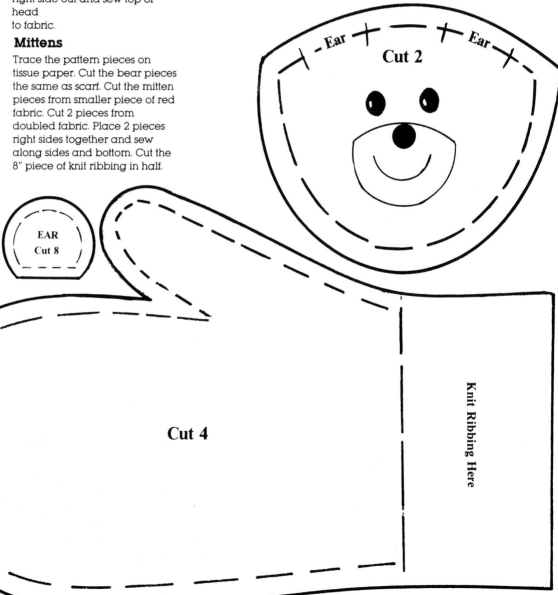

INNER EAR
Cut 4
Felt

Fold
SNOUT
Cut 1
Felt

EAR
Cut 8

Ear   Ear
Cut 2

Cut 4

Knit Ribbing Here

BEAR PURSE

Size
Approx. 7" x 8".

Materials
Light brown plush 11¾" x 21½". Small amounts of yellow felt. Yellow zipper 6" long. For lining: 8" x 20" of light brown cotton. Fiberfill. 57" length of tightly woven fabric webbing, 1¼" wide. Black plastic nose. 2 glass eyes. Brown embroidery thread.

Directions

Trace all pattern pieces onto tissue paper. Pin the tissue paper to the wrong side of fabric. From doubled plush fabric cut 1 center head piece and 1 snout piece on the fold. Also cut 2 back head pieces and 4 ear pieces. From single layer of plush fabric cut 2 side head pieces (1 reversed), and from the felt cut 2 inner ear pieces with ¼" seam allowance at lower edge. From the cotton fabric, cut all pieces the same as the plush fabric except the ears.

Purse
Sew felt inner ear pieces to right side of 2 ears. With right sides together sew outer ear seams, leaving the lower edge open. Turn right side out and stuff. Sew ears to side of head pieces where indicated. Sew center head piece and snout piece to side of head pieces, matching notches. Embroider the mouth in chain stitch with brown embroidery thread. Place eyes and nose. Sew the back center seam of head pieces, and then sew the back head pieces to side of head pieces, leaving the top open for zipper. Turn right side out.

Lining
Sew the lining pieces the same as the purse pieces. Insert the lining, wrong sides together. Stuff the front part of the purse through the top edge. Turn the seam allowance down on the top part of the back head piece and the top of the center head piece. Place the zipper here and sew by hand.

Finishing
Sew end pieces of the webbing behind each ear for shoulder strap.

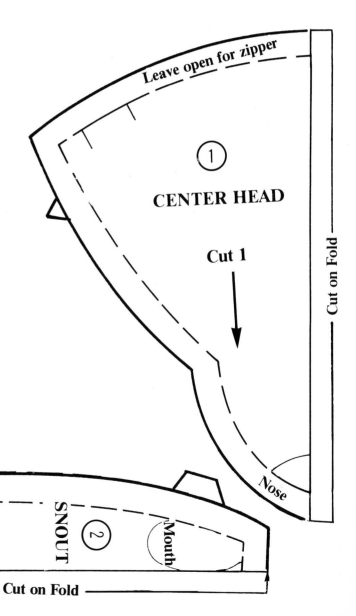

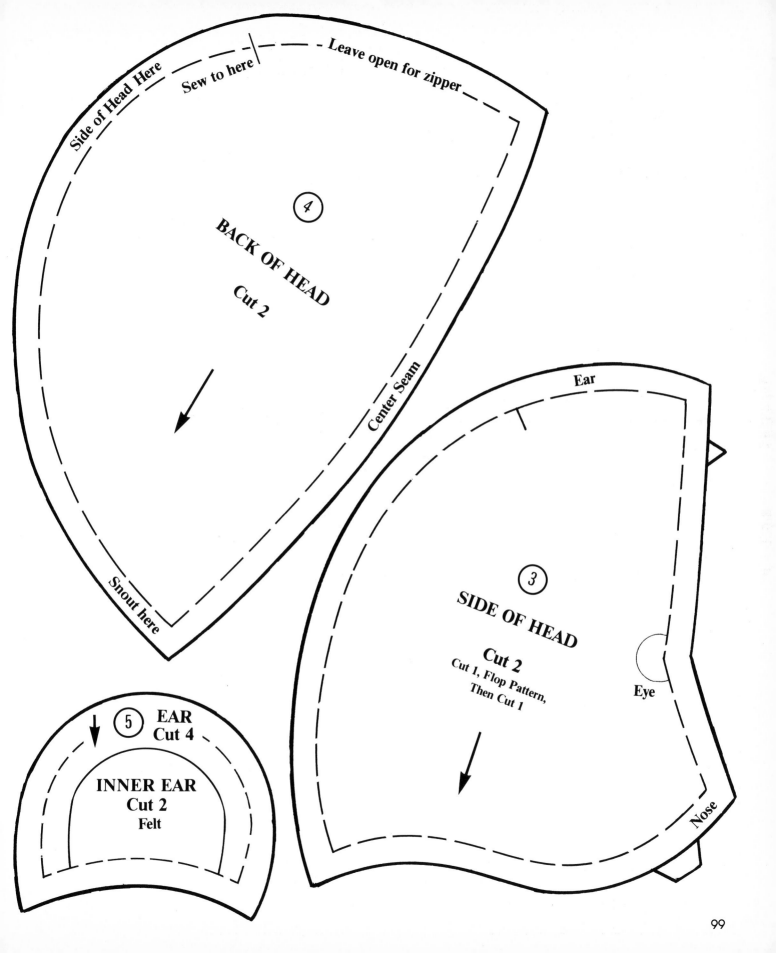

Side of Head Here

Sew to here

Leave open for zipper

④

BACK OF HEAD

Cut 2

Center Seam

Snout here

Ear

③

SIDE OF HEAD

Cut 2
Cut 1, Flop Pattern,
Then Cut 1

Eye

Nose

⑤ **EAR**
Cut 4

INNER EAR
Cut 2
Felt

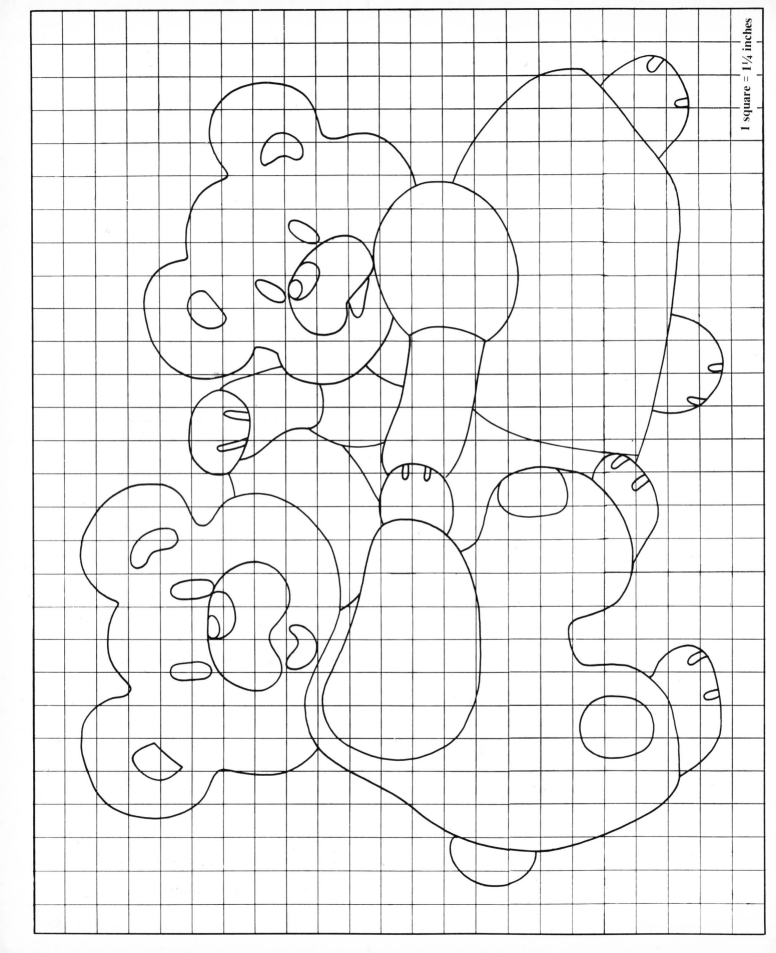

1 square = 1¼ inches

BEAR CUSHION

Size
31½" x 39¼".

Materials
2 yards of black cotton twill 60" wide. Foam rubber 33½" x 41½" wide and 1¼" thick. Interfacing 33½" x 41½" wide. For the appliqués: 22" x 18" medium brown felt; 8" x 12" dark brown felt. Small amounts of black and white felt. 4" x 6" dark brown leather. 16" x 20" pink and white polka dotted cotton. 20" x 20" turquoise cotton. 14" x 20" yellow striped fabric. 14" x 26" light brown cotton. 8" x 14" green cotton. 1½" wide pink and white plaid ribbon ¾ yard long. Tracing paper. Dressmakers' carbon paper.

Directions
Make a bear pattern on tracing paper in actual size using the graph as a guide (and each square is 1¼" x 1¼"). Make a pattern of the underlying bears and make separate patterns for all the pieces (clothes, eyes, etc.) Place the first pattern over the foam and cut out. Place the pattern over a piece of black cotton twill (33½" x 41½") and trace the outline of the piece and the outlines of the clothing, etc. using dressmakers' carbon paper. Cut out 1 piece with 2¾" seam allowance. This piece will be used for the base upon which you will sew the appliqués. Cut a 2nd piece from the black cotton twill for the backing with a ¼" seam allowance for the back. Cut the head, tail, and paws of the boy bear from medium brown felt without seam allowances. Cut the inner ears, claws, snout, mouth, and eyes from dark brown felt. Cut the nose from black felt and the highlight on the nose from white felt. With ¼" seam allowance, cut out the pants from turquoise cotton and the sleeves from striped cotton. Without seam allowances, cut out the pants and sleeves from interfacing.

Cut out the knee patches from leather, without seam allowances.

For the girl bear: with ¼" seam allowance, cut out the head and paws from the light brown cotton, the dress from polka dotted cotton, the sleeves from green cotton. Without seam allowances, cut out the same pieces in interfacing. Without seam allowances, cut out the inner ears, snout, eyes, and claws from brown felt, cut out the nose and tongue from dark brown felt, cut out the nose highlight from white felt.

Finishing
Appliqué: Place the fabric pieces (with seam allowances) over the interfacing wrong sides together. Fold the seam allowance over the interfacing and sew in place. Sew all the pieces of the clothing and body parts over the top piece of black cotton inside the indicated lines. Place the foam over the wrong side of the back piece of black cotton and place the appliquéd piece over the foam. Carefully sew the seams of the cotton twill by hand around the foam. Sew ribbon to the top of the girl's head.

BEAR HANGER

Size
Approx. 2¾" x 3¼".

Materials
Plywood 1/10" thick. Hobby paint. Paint brushes. Dressmaker's carbon paper. 8" long pink ribbon ⅛" wide. Blue high gloss paint. Glue. Primer. A plain wooden hanger. Jigsaw. Sandpaper.

Directions
Trace the bear motif on tissue paper and with carbon paper, then trace the motif on the plywood. Cut the bear from the plywood using the finest serrated blade on the jigsaw and sand the edges smooth. Paint the bear in the colors shown in the photo. Let it dry. Paint the back of the bear. Sand the hanger and paint with primer. Sand the hanger again. Paint the hanger blue and let dry thoroughly. Glue the bear to the hanger. Tie a bow around the bear's neck.

BEAR HAT RACK

Size

App. 7" x 19¼".

Materials

White Aida cloth 11¾" x 23½" with 10 thread group per inch. White flannel fabric 11¾" x 23½". DMC embroidery floss in the following colors: light brown #841, brown #840, dark brown #838, blue #825, pink #962, red #666, gray #318, medium brown #420, white, 4 wooden hooks. 4 screws. Pink and blue high gloss enamel. 7" x 19¼" chipboard. Picture hangers. 2 picture hanging eyes. Stapler.

Directions

Mark a rectangle 7" x 19¼" on the Aida cloth. Make sure all edges are even. Embroider the bears in cross-stitch working each cross-stitch over 1 thread group. Use 4 strands of embroidery floss for each cross-stitch and 3 strands of embroidery floss for the outline stitches. Begin with the standing skating bear (point A), 3¼" from the lower edge and 1¼" from the right side. Leave 49 threads between the middle of the bears. Continue embroidering bears as shown in photo. "Frame" the bears using 3 strands of pink ¼" from the edges of rectangle.

Finishing

Staple the white flannel to the chipboard, folding around edges. Staple the embroidery to the chipboard. Paint the wooden hooks and screw to front of rack as shown on photo. Attach the picture hanging eyes to the back.

Embroidery

Work the skates in gray #318, outline the shoes in medium brown #420, and the eyes in white. Outline the pants, sweaters, and mittens in blue. Work the lower edge of the sweaters in red #666; work the remaining outlines in dark brown #838.

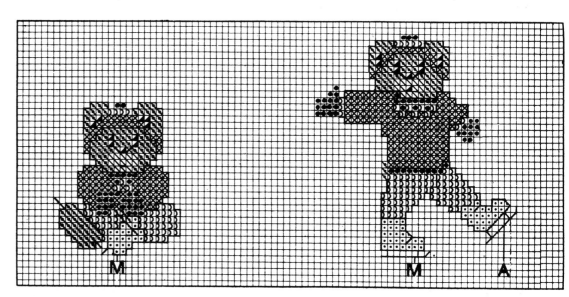

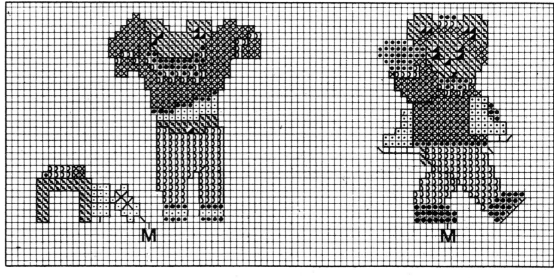

Key to Chart		
◩ Light brown #841	◪ Dark brown #838	⊠ Pink #962	⊡ White
◩ Medium brown #840	⊙ Blue #825	⬓ Red #666	

BEAR BACKPACK

Size
11½" x 12½".

Materials
14" x 48" of brown medium weight cotton blend fabric. Small piece of white suede. Fiberfill batting. Two ¾" grommets. 30" of brown cord. One 2" band of 2½" wide brown velcro. 40" of tightly woven brown cloth webbing. 4 "D" rings with straight edge 1¼" long. Brown and black embroidery thread. Tracing paper. For lining: 14" x brown lightweight cotton.

Directions

Trace the pattern pieces on tissue paper and pin the tissue paper to the wrong side of doubled fabric. From the medium weight cotton, light-weight cotton, and batting, cut 1 piece each of the front and back pieces on the fold. On single layer of fabrics, cut the flap and back pieces on the fold. On single layer of fabric, cut 4 ear pieces and cut 2 inner ear pieces from the suede fabric.

Attach the grommets to the front of the backpack where indicated for the cord to pass through. Mark and sew the darts on the front and front lining pieces. Place the front lining and front of backpack right sides together and sew the top seam. Turn right side out and sew a seam ¾" from the top edge to form a casing. Cut the brown cord in half and insert 1 end of each cord in the grommets and the other end at the side seams. Make a knot at the end at the cord so it won't slip back through the grommet. Fold two 6" pieces of the cloth webbing in half and thread 2 "D" rings on each loop. Sew both ends of the loop to indicated spots on the top edge of the back piece of the backpack, with curved part of rings pointing to the center.

Baste the front and back batting pieces to the wrong sides of backpack. Fold and cut in half the remaining pieces of cloth webbing. Sew ends to indicated spots on the bottom of the back piece. Then place the back and front pieces right sides together and sew around the sides and lower edges, leaving the top edge of the back free for the flap. Turn right side out. With right sides together, sew around sides and lower edges of back and front lining pieces. Place inside backpack.

Flap

Using dressmakers carbon, trace the face of the bear on the outside piece of the flap. Next, place the lower edge of the mouth 1" from the seam line of the flap. Embroider the eyes in brown, and the pupils and nose in a black satin stitch. Embroider the mouth in a black stem stitch. Sew on a piece of velcro to the flap lining at indicated spot. Baste the batting flap piece to the wrong side of flap. With right sides together, sew around outside edges, leaving the top edge open. Turn the flap right side out. Right sides together, sew the outside of flap to the outside of back. Hem the top of the back and flap linings and sew together.

Ears

Sew suede inner pieces to the right side of 2 outer ears. Place the outer ear pieces right sides together and sew around the top and side edges, leaving the lower edges open for turning. Turn right side out and stuff with fiberfill. Fold in lower edge and sew onto flap.

Finishing

Sew the second piece of velcro to the front of backpack.

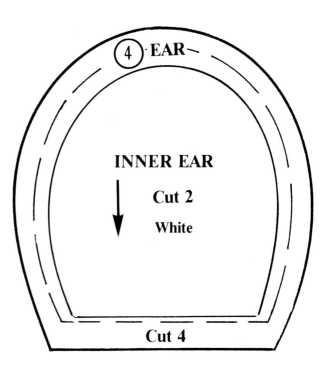

④ ·EAR~

INNER EAR

Cut 2

White

Cut 4

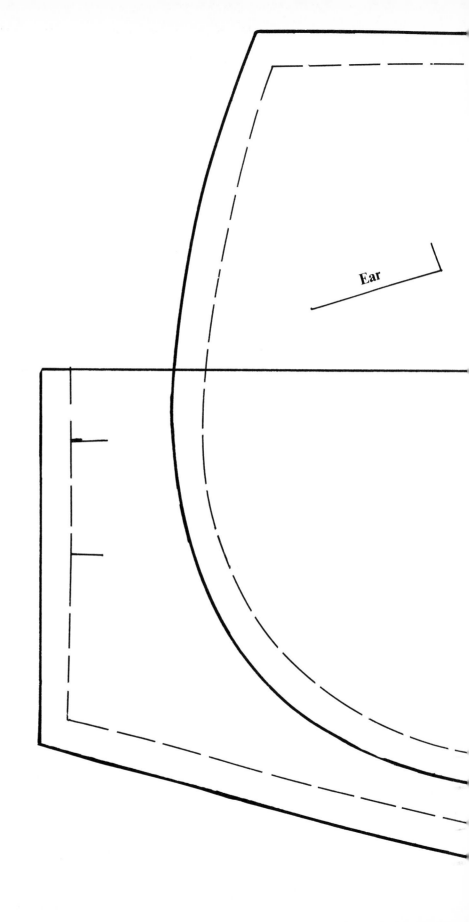

Ear

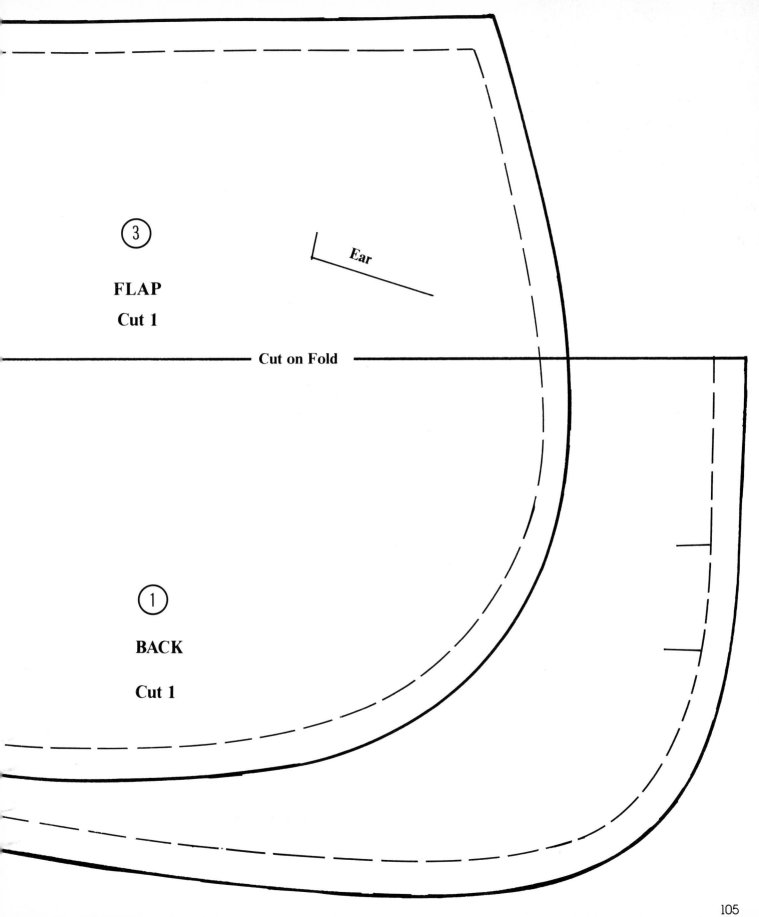

③

FLAP

Cut 1

Ear

Cut on Fold

①

BACK

Cut 1

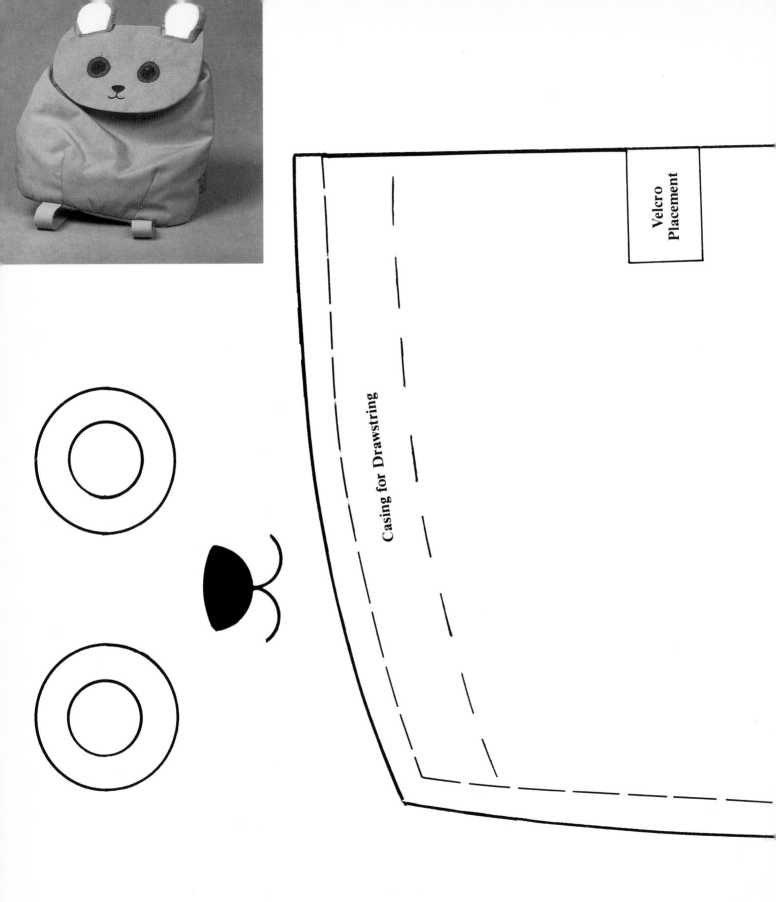

Velcro Placement

Casing for Drawstring

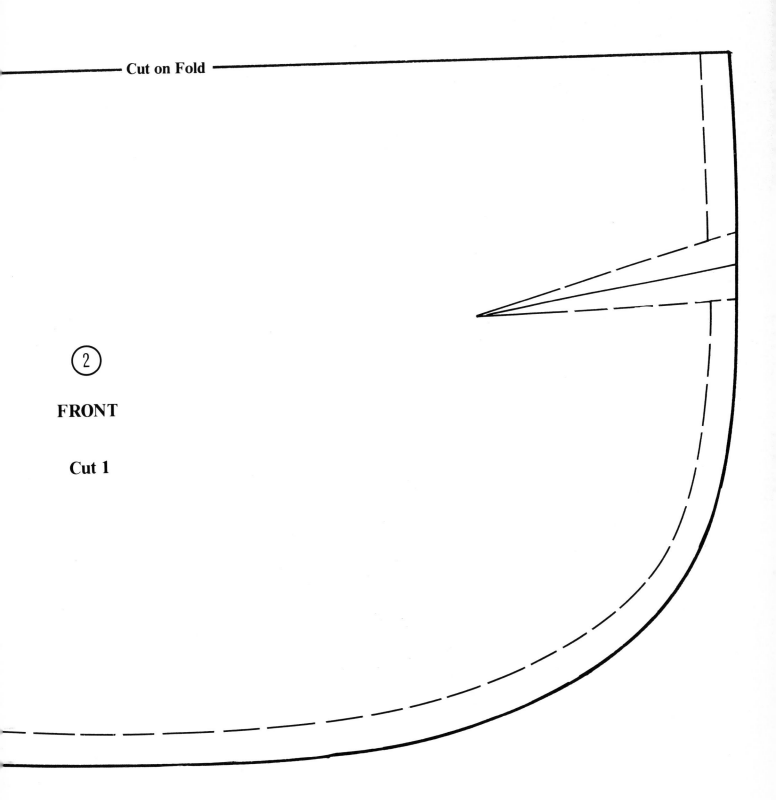

Cut on Fold

2

FRONT

Cut 1

BROWN BEAR RUG

Size
43¼" long.

Materials
71" x 55" dark brown plush fabric. 8" x 55" beige plush fabric. 2 glass eyes. Black felt for nose. 2 bags of fiberfill batting. Tracing or tissue paper.

Directions

Trace the pattern pieces on tracing paper. Pin the tracing paper to wrong side of the fabric. From dark brown fabric, cut 1 body piece (the pattern is for half the body), flip the pattern over and cut the other side, making the body all one piece. Repeat the process for bottom of the rug. Cut 2 ears, 2 side of head pieces (1 reversed), 2 tail pieces and 1 center headpiece. From beige fabric, cut 4 foot pads, 2 ears and 1 snout. From felt, cut 1 nose.

Head

Sew the sides of head to center head piece with right sides together. Turn right side out. Pin and sew on snout. Sew on eyes where indicated. Stuff the head and sew the opening closed. Sew the beige ears to the brown ears with right sides together, leaving lower edge open. Turn right side out. Fold in the lower ¼" edges and sew to head at indicated places. Pin the felt nose to the top of the snout opening. Fold and pin the edges to the head pieces. Sew the edges in place.

Body and Tail

Turn under seam allowance and sew on the beige foot pads to the underside of the body with wide zigzag stitches. With right sides together, sew the tail pieces around 3 sides, turn right side out, and stuff. Close by hand. Pin to indicated place on underside of body. Place under and upper sides of body with right sides together and sew around, leaving an opening at neck edge. Turn right side out and stuff. Sew on head.

Note: Depending on where and how your rug is used, you may want to use upholstery fabric on the underside of bear to keep it from sliding on floors.

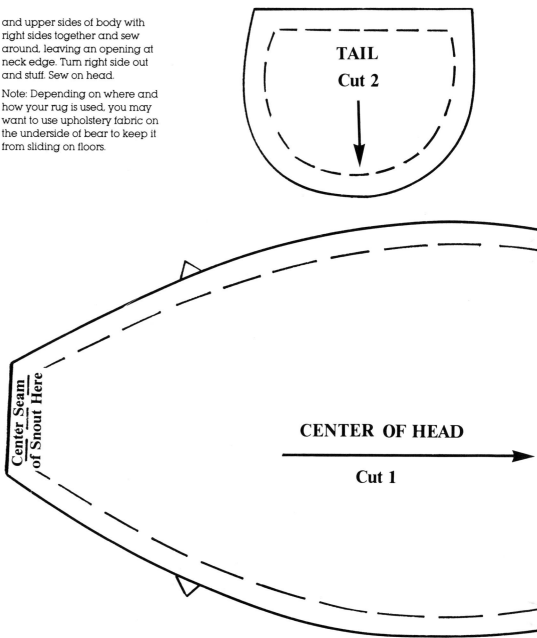

TAIL
Cut 2

Center Seam of Snout Here

CENTER OF HEAD

Cut 1

Enlarge Pattern Pieces 250%

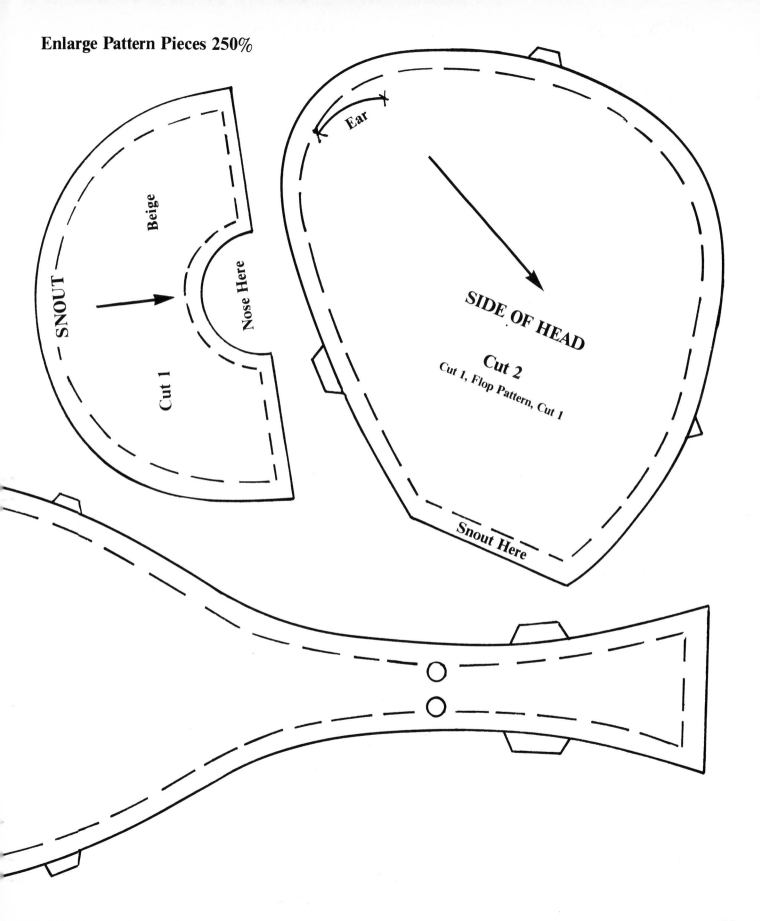

SNOUT

Beige

Cut 1

Nose Here

Ear

SIDE OF HEAD

Cut 2

Cut 1, Flop Pattern, Cut 1

Snout Here

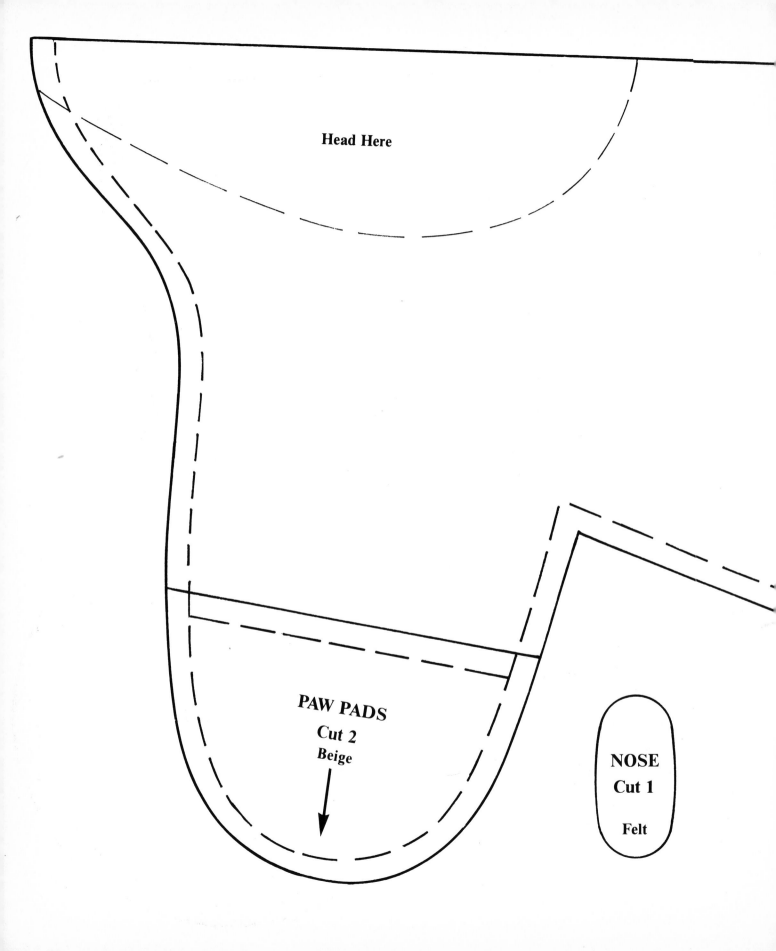

Head Here

PAW PADS
Cut 2
Beige

NOSE
Cut 1

Felt

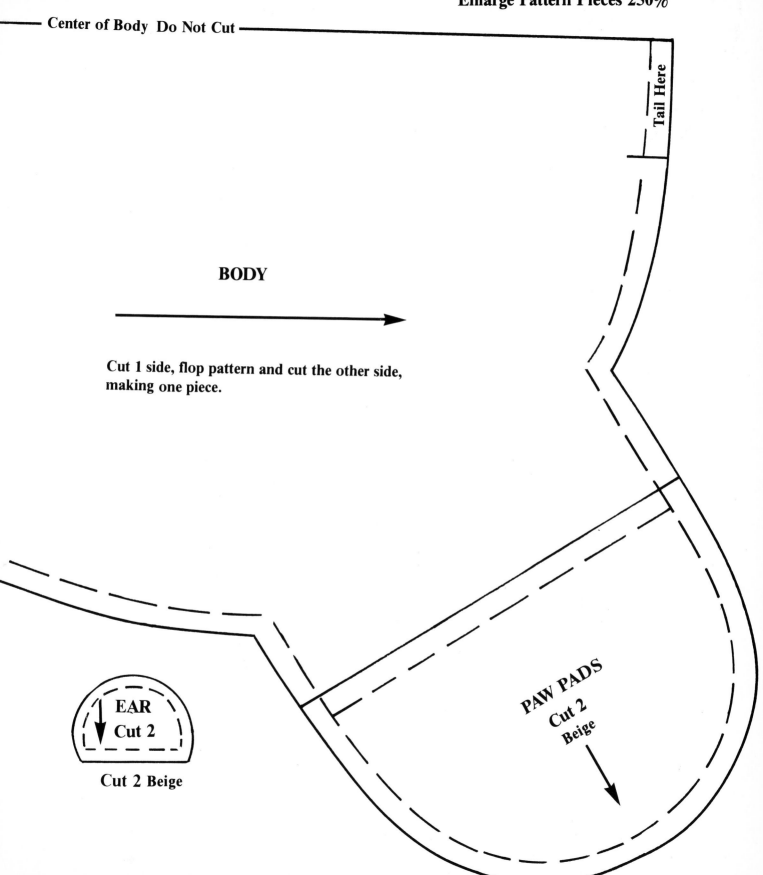

Enlarge Pattern Pieces 250%

Center of Body Do Not Cut

Tail Here

BODY

Cut 1 side, flop pattern and cut the other side,
making one piece.

EAR
Cut 2

Cut 2 Beige

PAW PADS
Cut 2
Beige

INDEX

A

Acrylic 13
Alpaca 13
Arms, construction of 18

B

Back stitch 16
Basting 13
Batting........................... 26
"Bear Backpack" 94, 103
Bear bodies, construction of 22
"Bear Cushion" 91, 100
"Bear Hanger" 92, 101
"Bear Purse" 90, 98
"Bear Rug" 95, 108
"Best Friend Bear" 57, 58
"Boris Bear" 96, 111
"Brown Bear" 34, 66
Buttons, used as joints........... 23

C

Calico 13
Chain stitch...................... 16
Construction 18-26
Corduroy 13
"Corduroy Bear" 53, 84
Cotter pins...................... 23
"Cross-Stitched Hat Rack" ... 93, 102
"Cuddly Bear" 29, 38
Curves, clipping of 14

D

Darts 14
Denim 13

E

Ears, construction of 21
Embroidery stitches 16
Eyes
    Choices 16
    Construction of 21
Excelsior......................... 26

F

Fabrics
    Choices 13, 14
    Durability 13
    Flame resistant............. 13
Felt 13
Fur
    Acrylic 13
    By-the-yard 13
    Cleaning of 14
    Fake 13
    Storing of................. 14
    Synthetic 13

G

Growlers......................... 26

H

Handbasting stitch 16
Hardboard disks 25
Heads, construction of 19, 20
History 6, 7
Holes, punching for cotter pins ... 24

J

Joints 23-26

K

Knits 13

L

Lace 13
Layouts, suggested 14
Legs, construction of............. 18

M

"Max" 36
Michtom, Morris 6
Modacrylic...................... 13
Mohair 13
Music boxes 27

N

Nap.......................... 13, 14
Noses 16
Nylon 13

O

"Olaf and Ollie" 30, 31, 42

P

"Panda Bear" 35, 62
"Petie Polar Bear" 33, 76
Pile 13
Polyester........................ 13

R

Remnants........................ 14
Right side....................... 13
Roosevelt, Theodore.............. 6

S

Safety 15, 16
Satin stitch 16
"Scarf/Mitten Set"............ 89, 97
Seam allowances 14
Squeakers 26
Stem stitch 16
Stitches, types of 16
Stuffing 26
Suede, synthetic 13
"Sweetheart Bear"........... 32, 50

T

Techniques, sewing 14, 15
Teddy's bears 6
Terry cloth 13
Threads......................... 15
Tracing 15
Tracing paper................... 13
"Treasure Bear" 55, 80

V

Velour 13
Velvet 13

W

Washers 25
Whip stitch...................... 16
Wrong side 14

BIBLIOGRAPHY

Bialosky, Peggy and Alan and Robert Tynes. **Making Your Own Teddy Bear**, 1982. New York: Workman Publishing Company, Inc.

Bialosky, Peggy and Alan. **The Teddy Bear Catalog**, 1980. New York: Workman Publishing Company, Inc.

Greenhowe, Jean. **Cuddly Toys and Dolls**, 1983. New York: Sterling Publishing Company, Inc.

Hall, Carolyn Vosburg. **The Teddy Bear Craft Book**, 1986. New York: Prentice Hall Press.

King, Doris. **Make Your Own Teddy Bears**, 1985. New York: Dover Publications, Inc.

Moore, Marsha Evans. **The Teddy Bear Book**, 1984. New York: Arco Publishing, Inc.

also: J. & P. Coats, 100 Embroidery Stitches